28586
26-03-92
AD.

The Innovative Society

Competitiveness in the 1990s

Bryne B. Purchase

Policy Review and Outlook, 1991
C.D. Howe Institute

C.D. Howe Institute publications are available from:

Renouf Publishing Company Limited, 1294 Algoma Road, Ottawa, Ontario K1B 3W8; telephone: (613) 741-4333; fax (613) 741-5439; and from Renouf's stores at: 61 Sparks Street, Ottawa (613) 238-8985; and 211 Yonge Street, Toronto (416) 363-3171

Institute publications are also available in microform from:

Micromedia Limited, 158 Pearl Street, Toronto, Ontario M5H 1L3

For trade book orders, please contact:

McGraw-Hill Ryerson Limited, 330 Progress Avenue, Scarborough, Ontario M1P 2Z5; telephone (416) 293-1911

This book is printed on partially recycled, acid-free paper

Canadian Cataloguing in Publication Data

HC
115
P87
1991

Purchase, Bryne Brock, 1944–
    The innovative society

(Policy review and outlook, ISSN 0826-9939 ; 1991)
Includes bibliographical references.
ISBN 0-88806-272-9

1. Canada – Economic policy – 1971–   .*
2. Canada – Commercial policy. 3. Canada – Social policy.
4. Canada – Politics and government – 1948–   .*
5. Competition, International. I. C.D. Howe Institute.
II. Title. III. Series.

HC115.P87 1991   338.971   C91-093640-4

Contents

Foreword

The year 1990 proved the old maxim that "it never rains, but it pours." The weather for 1991 does not appear to be much improved; Canadians are beset by recession, war, and constitutional and political strife.

In the midst of this turmoil, *The Innovative Society: Competitiveness in the 1990s* — the latest in the the C.D. Howe Institute's annual *Policy Review and Outlook* series — argues for perspective, for Canadians' seeing their situation clearly and for investing in themselves and in the quality of their public and private institutions.

Competitiveness is a popular notion in the business community just now, but its specific meaning for policy analysis is unclear. It is not a story that begins or ends with the exchange rate. *The Innovative Society* makes it clear that competitiveness is about the growth in output per employed person; that it is about continuously raising the real incomes of Canadians; and that it is about continued structural reform of the Canadian economy.

As the study points out, while competitiveness is a quality that is built into successful and enduring institutions, it is also a characteristic forged in the context of competing institutions. Competitiveness depends on competition. The challenge of good public policy is to create this environment.

Just as Canada's private sector must put competitiveness on its agenda, so must governments and government-funded institutions. *The Innovative Society* looks at this in the context of intergovernmental fiscal relations, the provision of health care and education, and mechanisms for reducing the excess burden of government social regulation.

Political and economic change in Canada is part of a much larger transformation in the world's political economy, and Canada's future policies must be developed in that broader understanding and context. In international trade, *The Innovative Society* reminds us of the need to press for the rule of law, not the law of the jungle of competing subsidies. And it argues that the way to build an innovative business community is to work on the fundamentals, on the basic infrastructure — not, for example, to guard jealously any specific asset from foreign takeover. In short, this year's *Policy Review and Outlook* reestablishes an old agenda for a new Canada.

The author, Bryne Purchase, is a Senior Policy Analyst at the Institute, and has also served as Assistant Deputy Minister, Ontario Ministry of Treasury and Economics, and Chief Economist of the Province of Ontario. The book was edited and desktop published by Barry A. Norris. Its preparation was also ably assisted by Céline Callender. As with all Institute publications, the conclusions presented here are the responsibility of the author and do not necessarily reflect the views of the Institute's members or Board of Directors.

Thomas E. Kierans
President and
Chief Executive Officer

1

Perspective, Competitiveness, and Competing Institutions

A Year of Discontinuity

This year's *Policy Review and Outlook* is being written at a time of enormous flux, both in domestic and international affairs. Public and private institutions, domestic and global, are under attack; they are seeking new relevance, new mandates, and renewed legitimacy in the eyes of their clients and constituents. In the process, they are restructuring, becoming smaller, and often suffering from a deep sense of malaise. Everywhere there is a recognition of the need for leadership and a genuine concern for the quality of that leadership.

In Canada, 1990 witnessed a fracture of the symmetry, structure, and progression of the recent past. Previous years had been characterized by a prolonged economic expansion and continual progress on a consistent federal economic policy agenda — an agenda rigorously examined in earlier editions of *Policy Review and Outlook*.[1] By the autumn of 1990, however,

---

1 See, for example, Edward A. Carmichael and Katie Macmillan, *Focus on Follow-through*, Policy Review and Outlook, 1988 (Toronto: C.D. Howe Institute, 1988).

public policy discussion no longer had the quality of business as usual. Something had changed dramatically; it no longer seemed meaningful to write a report card on the progress of the government's agenda.

Economic and Political Uncertainty

not that the actions of the past did not contain the seeds
day's discontent and malaise. In 1990, however, many
:rns coalesced and finally came to forefront of the public's
:iousness. They center on the arrival of recession and the
:al malaise and discontent following the collapse of the
1inute negotiations on the Meech Lake Accord, the Oka
ct, and the growing public hostility to federal economic
1s.

1e recession has resulted in a significant loss of employ-
In fact, job losses had already begun in the goods sector
in _е third quarter of 1989. The contraction was swift, especially in the manufacturing sector in Ontario. Service sector employment and income — often considered immune to recession — is now more fragile, and is declining after many months of consecutive gain.

Real estate values, both commercial and residential, have also fallen significantly in many parts of the country. This reversed the experience of previous years of rapid inflation, and it has also had deep psychological effects on household and business confidence.

The existence of high debt loads for households, businesses (particularly manufacturing), and government, and the increase in foreign debt loads for the country generally, make the burden and danger of recession for the security of Canada's financial structures that much greater. In particular, there was always concern that a recession would arrive before the federal government could make serious headway against the deficit. That has now happened.

The federal government is entering the second half of its second term. It has reached new lows in public opinion polls. Its deficit-reduction strategy has repeatedly failed to make acceptable headway, despite politically painful reductions in operating expenditures (excluding interest payments). Federal fiscal flexibility is severely constrained, adding to the fractiousness of provincial governments and the strong pressures for further political decentralization. In many ways, fiscal restraint has also fueled regional discontent.

The goods and services tax (GST), a major plank in the federal government's economic program, has been widely rejected by the public, and increased layoffs as a result of recession once again have heightened public anxiety about the economic impact of the Canada-U.S. Free Trade Agreement (FTA). As well, federal monetary policy has been the object of particularly strong criticism.[2]

The provinces are also feeling the fiscal squeeze of higher costs and recession-reduced revenues. The new Ontario government, for example, inherited an already deteriorating fiscal situation. The question now is: When that government deals with its own agenda, including pay equity, and confronts significant wage demands by public sector unions and professional groups, how much worse will its fiscal situation become?

The political scene is also fraught with uncertainty. In Quebec, the Bélanger-Campeau Commission will report by March 1991 on recommendations for that province's constitutional and political future. Other provinces will be similarly engaged. The creation of the Bloc Québécois and the surging popularity of the Reform Party in the West have added a new dynamic and corresponding new uncertainties to assessments of the future composition and party alignments of Parliament.

There has also been an apparent collapse of public support for government. A *Globe and Mail/CBC News* poll indicated

---

2 For an academic review, see Robert C. York, ed., *Taking Aim: The Debate on Zero Inflation*, Policy Study 10 (Toronto: C.D. Howe Institute, 1990).

that 64 percent of Canadians felt that their political leaders had neither a vision for the country's future nor an idea of how to achieve it.[3] Seventy-two percent felt that government did not care what they thought, and 67 percent felt that government was out of touch with their problems. Sixty percent trusted government to do what was right only some of the time, while another 16 percent hardly ever trusted government.

Theme: Perspective

Yet Canadians still have a strong belief in the institution of government. In the *Globe and Mail/CBC News* poll, 86 percent of respondents felt that, if government worked properly, it could solve most of the problems Canada faces. Moreover, people cared who they voted for, by an overwhelming margin: 70 percent rejected the proposition that it did not matter. On the question of the need for improvement in the system of government in Canada, 95 percent felt there was a need for improvement, while 34 percent were for a fundamental overhaul.

Perspective is always important, but it is especially crucial in these uncertain and turbulent times. It is essential not to let the speed of events dominate the senses and ultimately to dictate the course of action. In that respect, it is often useful to slow down, in the mind's eye, the pace of change and to reflect on the pattern of events that are unfolding.

The period leading up to the next federal election will be a critical one for Canadian public policy and, perhaps, also for Canada. Issues will be aired, views will be formed, decisions will be made, attitudes and positions will harden. These views will form the basis of competing visions of Canada and appropriate national policy.

---

3 See Hugh Winsor, "Malaise deals Tory support another blow," *Globe and Mail* (Toronto), October 29, 1990, p. A1.

The danger the C.D. Howe Institute sees in the next two years is that public opinion may be organized around the need to reverse previous policy directions, regardless of their rationale. The same impatience may emerge with respect to constitutional reform or Canada's relations with the international community — in particular, with the United States.

It is important for Canadians to maintain perspective on their current situation, in terms of past economic performance and the current recession. In many respects, the economy has performed strongly over the past several years. True, recession has struck, but the economy is already at its lowest point and the Institute is optimistic about a recovery later this year. The basis for this optimism is reviewed in Chapter 2.

Canadians also need perspective on where they stand in the international economy, on how the international economy functions, and on the implications for Canada's international trade, investment, and innovation policy. These issues are examined in Chapters 3 and 4.

Finally, Canada's current political malaise and institutional ferment should also be put in an international context. In a world filled with political and institutional change, Canada's situation is hardly unique. Recall that Europe's political institutions are undergoing profound change as well. The difference may be in whether one regards the present circumstance as an opportunity or an unrelieved threat. The Institute believes it could present opportunities for productive reform. Europeans went from "Eurosclerosis" — the persistence of high unemployment due to rigid social and economic structures — to the euphoria of "Europe 1992" in a few short years. Canadians can make similar psychological and practical leaps forward. This issue is addressed in Chapters 2 and 5.

As indicated earlier, this *Policy Review and Outlook* is not intended to be a report card on specific policy initiatives of the federal government, nor does it contain a host of detailed new policy proposals. Rather, it seeks to provide a more general perspective on the economic and political issues confronting the country. In doing so, it points out the directions that future reforms should take, and it establishes a new agenda for research and assessment over the coming year.

Theme: Competitiveness

A second basic theme of this year's *Policy Review and Outlook* is that Canada needs to continue to focus on strengthening the "competitiveness" of its public and private institutions.

The recession may sidetrack Canadians into endless debate about macroeconomic policy. Worse, it may cause us to lose sight of how much we have achieved in structural reform and how far we still have to go. Similarly, institutional malaise and political uncertainty may cause us to forget past achievements and our enormous economic prosperity, and to lose sight of our common aspirations for the future. It is essential that Canadians look beyond recession and political turmoil to a vision of the kind of society we wish to become. In the Institute's view, that society should be a competitive one.

Competitiveness as Public Policy

In terms of economic performance, the goal of competitiveness is measured by a high and continuously rising real standard of living; it is earned by constant improvements in labor productivity. Enhanced productivity comes about from having an increasing proportion of the economy involved in the production of higher-quality, higher-value-added, tradable goods and services. This is in addition to the traditional improvements in productivity that come from more efficient and larger-scale production.

In fact, however, as shown in Figure 1, real labor income per worker fell during the 1977–87 period. This represented

Figure 1

Real Labor Income per Employed Person in Canada, 1967–89
(annual percentage change)

percent

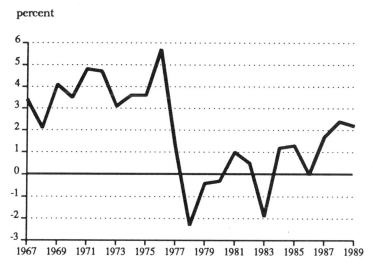

Source: Statistics Canada.

ten lost years, because it followed increases in the previous decade of 3.5 percent per annum. Only since 1987 has real labor income per worker begun to grow again, averaging a promising 2.1 percent annual growth to 1989. At the same time, the Canadian labor market has become increasingly polarized into those with "good" jobs and those with "bad" jobs, with corresponding income disparities.[4] And a rising burden of national and international debt could exacerbate inter-generational political conflicts over future repayment of this debt. A competitiveness agenda, by increasing real income per worker, is meant to address both of these issues.

---

4 See Economic Council of Canada, *Good Jobs, Bad Jobs: Employment in the Service Economy* (Ottawa: Supply and Services Canada, 1990).

Competitiveness as Economic Security

In public policy discussion, there is often a gap between the attitudes, values, and advice of economic experts and those of business and the general public. Ultimately that gap must be closed, not only because experts are not always right, but, especially, because no reform initiative can be undertaken successfully without the understanding and consent of the broader public.

Part of the problem with the theme of "competitiveness" in public policy is that the term defies common understanding. It may be that economic security strikes a better note for Canadians, especially in a recession. Indeed, competitiveness as a goal may sound like seeking competition for its own sake; yet few subscribe to this in their business or personal life. In their economic activities, people seek income, wealth, and economic security. The connection with competitiveness is that, in a global economy — indeed, in any market economy — the greatest security, the only lasting security, is found in being competitive.

Theme: Competitive and Competing Institutions

The essential promise of an open global economy is the continuous improvements in material welfare it can bring to its participants. The tremendous economic progress of Germany and Japan, as they were encouraged to participate in the postwar expansion of the international economy under the General Agreement on Tariffs and Trade (GATT), is witness to that fact. So too, in reverse fashion, is the apparent impending collapse of the Soviet imperial state for its gross failure to deliver continuous improvements in economic, social, and environmental welfare.

The Institute believes strongly in the need for Canadians to participate fully in the international economy as a way to enhance their real incomes. But the other side of participating in the global economy is the fact that it exposes Canadians to competition from distant places. Modern telecommunications and transportation have increased not only the extent but also the speed with which this exposure is manifest. Canadians cannot insulate themselves from the forces of global competition without diminishing the benefits of global integration. But it is not simply a choice between one or the other — Canadians can participate actively in building new international institutions designed to secure benefits for all.

Of course, there will always be external forces beyond our control, but there is also something internal — some quality built into Canada's communities and institutions — that is equally powerful. Indeed, this quality, this characteristic, sustains us through the inevitable periods of misfortune and allows us to seize opportunities and make the best of them. That quality is what is meant here by "competitiveness". There are different measures of competitive performance, but competitiveness can only be understood as a characteristic that must be built into Canadian institutions, values, and society.

A competitive society is built on competitive, and competing, institutions. The competitiveness of public institutions and private corporations matters. Their ability to respond to crisis, on the one hand, and to use success to build the foundations of greater success, on the other, are central elements.

The things that make an institution — or, ultimately, a society — competitive are built into its values, its organizational structure, and the quality of its internal and external relationships. True competitiveness is also an enduring feature. It is not dominated by short-term gain; instead, it focuses on what is necessary to survive and prosper over the long term. It emphasizes continual reinvestment in the quality of the institution. It maintains an incentive structure that efficiently helps the institution to reach its goals. Above all, competitiveness depends on the ability to innovate and the willingness to accept change.

Competitive institutions do not just happen. They are part of a larger political and economic structure that encourages competition. Institutions must have not only the opportunity to succeed, but also the pressure to succeed. Public policy can help to enhance and maintain that climate. The need to maintain an economic and political climate and corresponding structures that are conducive to competition, challenge, and innovation is an essential feature of competitiveness.

Change and Social Acceptance

An agenda based on competitiveness does not necessarily involve more government or new subsidies. Instead, it should focus on structural, institutional, and legal reform, and on reordering the priorities of public and private agencies and policies. It should emphasize quality and service to the consumer and taxpayer.

In all of this, the Institute is aware of the need for measured progress. Seeking competitiveness through structural reform is itself an extraordinarily divisive exercise, and the public's tolerance for rapid change is by no means inexhaustible. The intense political battles over the Canada-U.S. FTA, the GST, and the reform of unemployment insurance (UI) are all recent examples of how difficult this process can be. Each, however, adds to Canada's long-term competitiveness and, ultimately, to the country's economic security and political cohesion. Yet, the short-term political bruising is great, and sometimes dangerously so.

Enduring public policy requires that there be at least acceptance of, if not enthusiasm for, the long-term efficacy of public initiatives. Some people despair that this is possible. Good economic policy is often simply too tough for the public to accept. But to believe this is to reject the ultimate compatibility between democracy and economic progress through mixed capitalist societies. The Institute cannot accept that proposition.

Critical to building acceptance is that structural reforms not brutalize the social contract. Those who personally lose, so that society might gain, must be compensated. A generous program of adjustment assistance is an essential element of any fundamental reform process, otherwise reform might be blocked or even reversed.[5] The best-managed private companies understand this; so must government.

But people must also have hope for their future. They must be afforded the opportunity to invest in themselves and to build for themselves. Values, education, skills training, and health are essential to that process. It may sound trite, but people will always be Canada's ultimate resource and the source of its ultimate comparative advantage.

Innovative Government

Many of the major structural reforms to date — such as the GST, the FTA, or UI reforms — have required the public to accept change. There is a widespread feeling, however, that government and government institutions must change as well. Opinion polls suggest that the public is against increased taxes, but in favor of increased spending on some government programs. One can use this apparent inconsistency as an excuse to reject the validity of public attitudes. But the polls also show that the public believes there is waste and inefficiency in government. While this inefficiency may be over-

---

5 The need for such assistance was recognized by the Macdonald Commission in its discussion of adjustments to Canada-U.S. free trade. See Royal Commission on the Economic Union and Development Prospects for Canada, *Report,* 3 v. (Ottawa: Supply and Services Canada, 1985).

estimated, it is not inconsistent with the notion of enhanced service without tax increases.

In public policy terms, a competitiveness agenda is not just about policies to foster competitiveness in private enterprise; government-funded institutions are very much a part of such an agenda. It is not just about how government will help others to become more competitive, nor is it just, or even primarily, about a new industrial policy. Rather, it is about how government will become competitive in turn. If they are to survive, public policies and institutions must serve some long-term functional purpose, and they must do so in a way that is better than competing private institutions and options. Therefore, an important theme in this year's *Policy Review and Outlook* is the need for *all* levels of government and public institutions to become competitive, efficient, and innovative.

Provincial governments, municipalities, school boards, and hospitals now account for much of the delivery of public goods in Canada, and for an increasing amount of social regulation. To leave them out would be to miss much of what government really does. Accordingly, reform increasingly must focus on the policies and operations of these public institutions, particularly as Canadians come to identify more closely with them than with institutions at the national level.

Government must also be encouraged to become more efficient in its choice of policy tools. For example, government is less efficient when it imposes not only a regulatory standard but also the manner in which it is to be achieved.

Finally, competitiveness means addressing the question of which level of government can most efficiently and inventively meet Canadian's needs and aspirations for public goods and services, for coherent regulatory structures, for redistributive policies, and for various types of social insurance.

Government must be structured such that it encourages competition and efficiency not only in the private sector (for example, through uniform standards and regulations), but also in its own provision of services (for example, through efficient intergovernmental fiscal relations). Different levels of government must be allowed to accept the accountability for taxing what they choose to spend, and to spend according to the priorities of their constituents.

These themes are all central elements of this year's *Policy Review and Outlook.*

2

Maintaining Perspective: The Current Malaise

Perspective is always important, but especially so in the midst of Canada's current political and economic malaise. Perspective helps to avoid panic responses. This chapter argues the need to maintain perspective on:

- Canada's recent economic performance and policy record;
- the onset of recession and short-term problems of cost competitiveness relative to the United States; and
- the nation's current political turmoil.

A Perspective on Recent Policy

What is especially perplexing about Canada's current disarray is that it follows on both a consistent federal public policy agenda and a prolonged expansion of economic activity that compares favorably with the records of other countries in the Organisation for Economic Co-operation and Development (OECD). The current disarray also follows a period of significant policy success, judged by international standards: Canada's international competitiveness ranking went from seventh out of 23 OECD countries in 1986, to fourth in 1989.

A Consistent Policy Framework

As a package, the proposals contained in the federal government's 1984 economic agenda paper, the Canada-U.S. FTA, and the tax reform initiatives represented a coherent and consistent framework for increasing Canadian competitiveness and productivity.[1]

Not all of the proposed changes were accomplished. Of those that were, there was not always agreement on their design or details. Nonetheless, they are expected to bring permanent real income gains to Canadians. The Department of Finance estimates that structural reforms will raise potential output growth from 2.75 percent to a range of 3.25 to 3.5 percent during the 1990–95 period.[2] What is important, however, is not the specific estimate, but the direction of change.

Improved Economic Performance

These prospective improvements follow a very strong economic performance in real output and employment growth. Over the 1983–89 period, Canada's real output growth exceeded that of every other Group-of-Seven (G-7) country except Japan (see Figure 2). In terms of employment growth, only the United States performed better.

Part of this performance was, of course, related to the depth of the recession in 1981–82. Moreover, the expansion was not

---

1 See Hon. Michael H. Wilson, *A New Direction for Canada: An Agenda for Economic Renewal* (Ottawa: Department of Finance, November 1984). These initiatives were outlined and reviewed in Edward A. Carmichael, Katie Macmillan, and Robert C. York, *Ottawa's Next Agenda*, Policy Review and Outlook, 1989 (Toronto: C.D. Howe Institute, 1989).

2 Hon. Michael H. Wilson, *The Budget: Canada's Economic Performance and Prospects* (Ottawa: Department of Finance, February 20, 1990), p. 52.

Figure 2

Growth of Real Gross Domestic Product and Employment in the Group-of-Seven Countries, 1983–89
(annual percentage change)

percent

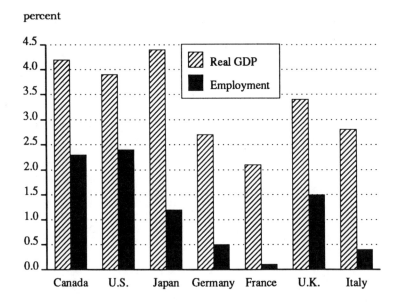

Source: Department of Finance.

felt uniformly across the country — high unemployment persisted in many areas. Nonetheless, the momentum was in the right direction and, with respect to major reforms such as the FTA, the regions of highest unemployment most strongly supported the federal government's economic initiatives. Reforms such as dismantling of the National Energy Program and the creation of the Atlantic Opportunities Agency and the Western Diversification Program were successful in responding to regional concerns and past grievances.

Canada's improved economic performance in the 1980s gained recognition in the international business community.

Table 1
How Canada Ranks in Competitiveness
Relative to 23 Industrialized Countries, 1986–90

Factor	1986	1989	1990
Dynamism of economy	7	3	5
Industrial efficiency	8	4	13
Market orientation	7	4	5
Financial dynamism	7	11	10
Human resources	4	2	3
State interference	8	3	6
Natural endowments	3	2	2
International orientation	12	14	15
Future orientation	9	15	16
Socio-political stability	7	6	8
Overall	*7*	*4*	*5*

Source: IMEDE and the World Economic Forum, *The World Competitiveness Report*, various years.

As illustrated in Table 1, a dynamic growth environment and a better cost performance significantly improved Canada's ranking from 1986 to 1989 in the prestigious *World Competitiveness Report.*

As well, a large part of Canada's improved ranking came from factors directly related to public policy changes affecting areas that the Report refers to as "dynamics of the market", "state interference", and "socio-political stability". Areas where the ranking fell back were in "financial dynamism" — relating to factors such as fiscal deficits, low savings rates, and high interest rates — and in "international" and "future orientation" — relating to the narrow market concentration of Canada's exports and low levels of innovative activity. Unfortunately, in 1990, Canada lost ground in nearly all of these areas, and its overall rank dropped from fourth to fifth.

Public Rejection

Despite these significant economic achievements, the current mood of the public is to reject the federal government's economic program. Is this a rejection of the goal of these reforms? Surely not. Is it necessarily a rejection of specific policies? On this score, there may be greater debate. But as indicated above, the Institute does not believe this is the case. Why, then, is there such public discontent?

The source of this discontent may well be more deeply rooted in the federal government's failure to acknowledge, in a symbolic and significant way, the need for adjustment assistance in the face of what the public perceives as a major structural reform — as the FTA, for example, certainly is. The government itself has also failed to become visibly a part of the reform agenda — as perhaps best exemplified by its continual inability to reduce the deficit, despite the priority it has publicly attached to that goal. Finally, there is the issue of timing. The arrival of cost pressures, tight monetary policy, and then recession has clouded the relationship between the effects of structural reforms — such as the FTA — and those of cyclical performance. Fortunately, if the monetarists are correct, the worst may be over — an issue to which we now turn.

A Perspective on Recession

The 1981–82 recession left a large gap between actual and potential output in the Canadian economy. By 1987, that gap had closed. The economy actually grew beyond potential in 1988, and close to potential in 1989.[3] Wage and cost pressures began to emerge and some slowdown became inevitable.

---

3 Wilson, *The Budget*, p. 24.

International Cost Competitiveness

Particularly worrisome in recent years has been the growth in Canada's unit labor costs relative to those in the United States. As Table 2 illustrates, compensation costs — including both wage and nonwage benefits — have been rising considerably faster in Canada than in the United States, but productivity gains in the Canadian business sector have not kept pace, especially in manufacturing.

In the absence of stronger federal fiscal restraint — or tougher provincial fiscal restraints, for that matter — the Bank of Canada tightened monetary policy in an effort to deal with the potential for higher inflation and, in fact, to achieve an even lower rate of inflation. The goal of price stability, which is estimated to be slightly less than 2 percent annual consumer price inflation, became the policy target.[4]

The use of monetary policy to aim for a domestic inflation target has meant that higher short-term interest rates have resulted in further increases in the Canadian dollar exchange rate. The higher dollar has made Canada's short-term cost competitiveness *vis-à-vis* the United States deteriorate even more sharply. In fact, for manufacturing, Canada's relative position in 1989 was the worst since the 1950s. From a business perspective, then, the pressure comes from all sides: rising wage demands, higher interest rates, and a higher dollar. Canadian corporate profits have reflected this squeeze.

Monetary policy's effect on the dollar is not the only factor at work. Substantially increased government regulation, especially at the provincial level — in areas such as the environment, health and safety, pensions, and employment standards — has also meant increasing costs. In many instances, the new regulations were conceived before the conclusion of the Can-

---

4 See David E.W. Laidler and William B.P. Robson, *Money Talks — Let's Listen!*, C.D. Howe Institute Commentary 26 (Toronto: C.D. Howe Institute, 1991).

Table 2

Trends in Cost Competitiveness in Canada and the United States, 1987–89

(average annual percentage change, unless otherwise noted)

	Unit labor costs (U.S. dollars)	Unit labor costs in domestic currency	Hourly labor compensation	Output per hour
	Business sector			
Canada				
1987	$9.1	4.1%	5.4%	1.3%
1988	12.5	4.4	6.0	1.5
1989	10.6	6.4	8.2	1.7
1987–89	*10.7*	*5.0*	*6.6*	*1.5*
United States				
1987	2.6	2.6	3.9	1.2
1988	3.0	3.0	4.8	1.7
1989	4.4	4.4	5.5	1.1
1987–89	*3.3*	*3.3*	*4.7*	*1.3*
	Manufacturing			
Canada				
1987	7.3	3.3	4.1	0.7
1988	11.2	3.2	4.9	1.7
1989	10.3	6.2	8.5	2.2
1987–89	*9.9*	*4.2*	*5.8*	*1.5*
United States				
1987	−1.0	−1.0	2.7	3.7
1988	1.3	1.3	3.6	3.0
1989	2.2	2.2	4.2	2.0
1987–89	*0.8*	*0.8*	*3.5*	*2.7*

Sources: For Canadian data, Statistics Canada, *Aggregate Productivity Measures*, Cat. no. 15-204 (Ottawa, 1990). For U.S. data, United States, Department of Labor, Bureau of Labor Statistics, *News: Productivity and Costs*, first quarter 1990; and United States, *Economic Report of the President Transmitted to the Congress February 1990* (Washington, D.C.: U.S. Government Printing Office, 1990).

ada-U.S. FTA negotiations, and while the Canadian dollar, under pressure from collapsing commodity prices, was in the range of 73 to 77 cents U.S. At those exchange rates, Canadian manufacturers were highly competitive relative to their counterparts in neighboring U.S. states. This serendipitous cost competitiveness may have muted the initial response of the business community to the cost implications of increased regulatory activity.

As the dollar has swung around, however — again, largely for reasons unrelated to underlying manufacturing cost competitiveness — regulatory compliance costs have become a more serious concern. Yet they are now built into the cost structure. Restoring short-term cost competitiveness is then achieved either through reducing employment or through lowering wage rates — and the latter is notoriously difficult to do. The net effect, then, of higher and higher levels of mandated costs may be to make employment in the traded goods sector even more sensitive to exchange-rate increases.

The Political Economy of Price Stability

As a result of the higher dollar and higher interest rates, the Bank of Canada has drawn widespread public criticism. The Bank's policy has also generated a debate among economists over the appropriate target of monetary policy — some believe it should be to achieve a rate of inflation no higher than that in the United States.[5] As well, the debate has encompassed those who would adopt a fixed exchange rate (at a lower value) and those who would maintain the current, flexible rate.

In fact, however, neither fixing the exchange rate nor letting it float resolves the regional and political bluntness of monetary

---

5 See Pierre Fortin, "Can the Costs of an Anti-Inflation Policy Be Reduced?" in Robert C. York, ed., *Taking Aim: The Debate on Zero Inflation*, Policy Study 10 (Toronto: C.D. Howe Institute, 1990), pp. 135–172.

effects. The stabilization target is achieved in the aggregate, not with the plight of any individual region, industry, firm, or, for that matter, household in mind. In the final analysis, the real issues boil down to, first, whether the policy objective of price stability is too costly in terms of lost output and investment to achieve, given the benefits; and, second, whether there was any viable alternative to the use of monetary policy.

One view argues that the costs outweigh the benefits, and that potentially the costs are very long lasting.[6] In particular, this view holds that exchange-rate appreciation, stemming from high short-term Canadian interest rates, could not have come at a worse time given the need to gain new U.S. markets under the FTA. The effect may be particularly onerous on small and medium-sized firms, which are likely to be Canadian owned, with lower plant productivity levels than the multinationals, and which are already facing major distribution barriers in their attempts to develop U.S. markets.

The opposing view focuses on the key role that price stability plays in enhancing the long-term efficiency and distributional equity of the economy.[7] Also, strong-currency countries are high-productivity performers.

On the question of alternatives to monetary policy, the absence of greater fiscal restraint, either federally or provincially, has already been noted. Such restraint would have made the Bank of Canada's job easier. There is, of course, no incentive for voluntary restraint unless one could be assured that others would act similarly.

---

6 See Robert F. Lucas, "The Case for Stable, But Not Zero, Inflation," in York, ed., *Taking Aim*, pp. 65–80.

7 These arguments were set out in detail by David Laidler, "Monetary Policy," in Thomas E. Kierans, ed., *Getting It Right*, Policy Review and Outlook, 1990 (Toronto: C.D. Howe Institute, 1990), pp. 6–23. A number of other economists who have studied the costs and benefits of price stability in detail have reached the same conclusion. See, for example, Peter Howitt, "Zero Inflation as a Long-Term Target for Monetary Policy," in Richard G. Lipsey, ed., *Zero Inflation: The Goal of Price Stability*, Policy Study 8 (Toronto: C.D. Howe Institute, 1990), pp. 67–108.

With regard to other policy options, the Economic Council of Canada has recently reopened the issue of finding other institutional mechanisms that would help to ensure that compensation did not get out of line with this country's productivity performance.[8] Institutional reform of the wage-setting process along these lines, if it could be made effective, would contribute to Canada's long-term competitiveness. Unfortunately, most proposals require fundamental structural reform, which, even if achievable, would take a long time to implement and could not have any impact on the current situation.

Moreover, such proposals typically depend on a tripartite agreement between big business, unions, and government to voluntarily restrain themselves, even though they may not be the primary victims of a policy of monetary restraint. Any larger, more encompassing groupings would have to be constructed on highly fragmented business and labor constituencies in Canada. No constituency could speak with one voice. Accordingly, the potential for success remains limited at this stage.

In addition, one should not underestimate the importance of a stable monetary environment in producing harmony among competing groups in society. Uncertainty about future inflation may increase the degree of intergroup tension and hostility, and make tripartite-style reforms more problematic to implement. On balance, the Institute believes that the current monetary policy is appropriate and is most conducive to Canada's long-term competitiveness.

The Severity of the Recession

Whatever the pros and cons of current Canadian monetary policy, the experiment is well under way and the outcomes are

---

8 Economic Council of Canada, *Transitions for the '90's,* Twenty-Seventh Annual Review (Ottawa: Supply and Services Canada, 1990). See also Fortin, "Can the Costs of an Anti-Inflation Policy Be Reduced?" in York, ed., *Taking Aim,* pp. 135–172.

largely set. Those outcomes have to do with the degree to which inflation will slow and the length of the current recession. On both counts, these issues have to be seen in a North American context. The output and inflation performance of the U.S. economy is also central to questions of the depth of Canada's recession and the comparative short-term cost performance of the Canadian economy.

In the absence of a serious recession in the United States, and given current indications from Canadian monetary policy, there is a good chance that Canada's recession will bottom out by mid-1991. The Institute also expects that Canada's underlying price and cost performance will improve significantly. Certainly, most forecasters are expecting economic recovery by 1992.

A serious recession in the United States — perhaps associated with a major financial crisis — would, however, further exacerbate Canada's own domestic slowdown. At present, most forecasters believe that there is little risk of recession in Europe or Japan, and continued moderate growth is expected in these countries. In any case, the immediate key to Canadian export performance is U.S. economic performance. The consensus of private U.S. forecasters currently calls for two quarters of negative growth in the U.S. economy, straddling 1990 and 1991. Again, monetary authorities will be the key players.

There is a view that the U.S. Federal Reserve will assiduously avoid anything beyond a mild recession, even if that means accepting higher inflation.[9] The reason is the very precarious position of the U.S. financial sector, primarily as a result of regional collapses in real estate values. this position has been made even more uncertain by the onset of recession nationally and the extremely high level of corporate indebtedness following the binge of takeovers, leveraged buyouts, junk-

---

9 For a discussion of these issues, see Benjamin M. Friedman, "Financial Fragility and the Policy Dilemma," *Challenge*, July/August 1990, pp. 7-16.

bond financing, and equity repurchases. The bailout of savings and loan institutions after the failure of the U.S. Federal Savings and Loan Insurance Corporation is already adding a huge additional burden to U.S. taxpayers. Now, the Federal Deposit Insurance Corporation (FDIC) fund for banks is down to an extremely low percentage of insured deposits. Bank failures beyond those currently forecast by the FDIC would exhaust that fund as well.

In dealing with a potential financial crisis in the United States, the Fed, as lender of last resort, has a higher priority than inflation: to preserve the financial structure of the U.S. economy. The most probable bet, then, is that the United States will accept a higher rate of inflation if necessary, in order to keep its economy out of serious recession.

In Canada, however, the Bank of Canada's restrictive monetary stance has continued to put downward pressure on inflation. As David Laidler noted in last year's *Policy Review and Outlook*, price stability requires annual money growth rates of around 3 percent for the M1 monetary aggregate and 5 percent for M2.[10] In mid-1990, it appeared as though there had been a policy overshoot — that the Bank had become too restrictive even to achieve its own price-stability goals. The growth of M1 actually dropped well below the required ranges, foreshadowing the economy's recent pronounced weakness. Since August, however, the monetary aggregates have rebounded. At present, the growth of M1 and M2 — after allowing for the distorting effect of Canada Savings Bond redemptions — appears to be on a path consistent with continued disinflation, while allowing for a rebound in real output and, to a lesser degree, employment.[11]

---

10 See Laidler, "Monetary Policy," in Kierans, ed., *Getting It Right*, p.16. M1 consists of currency plus chequable deposits with the chartered banks. The broader M2 monetary aggregate includes personal savings accounts and nonpersonal notice deposits held by the chartered banks.

11 For a discussion of these issues and this forecast, see Laidler and Robson, *Money Talks — Let's Listen!*.

It will be important for the Bank of Canada to encourage continued expansion of the money supply at a steady, non-inflationary rate over the coming months. In light of the pronounced weakness in the economy since early 1990, the recent rebound in money growth should be seen as a welcome indication that output and employment in the first half of 1991 may be stronger than is widely forecast. In addition, unless there is a new, sustained surge of money growth, inflation will continue to decline — notwithstanding the temporary effects of the GST and higher oil prices — through the next two years. It could fall to the 2–2.5 percent range by the end of 1992, which is well below the current range expected by other forecasters. Such a low rate of consumer price inflation would represent a strong base for renewed real income growth.

In sum, given the vulnerability of the United States to a decision to inflate — to avoid financial collapse and a severe recession — and also given Canada's current monetary regime, this country should emerge from recession with a much improved relative cost position. This will provide a great deal more potential for a sharp decline in short-term interest rates.

A Perspective on Political Turmoil

Canada's current political turmoil should be seen in the context of a more general worldwide political upheaval. In that perspective, Canada's problems are not necessarily a unique failing on the part of its politicians or institutions.

The world is in the midst of a profound political and economic transformation. The apparent disintegration of the Soviet empire, Europe 1992, the unification of Germany, the beginnings of a Japanese-dominated Western Pacific trade bloc, the continued development of a North American bloc (potentially including Central and South America), and the rise of intense regional, national, and subnational coalitions and governments throughout the world share a common root.

Political institutions are being transformed and new ones considered, in response to global economics.[12]

Recent developments in the international economy are rooted in the unparalleled wealth-creating ability of globalized free market integration. This is coupled with the disintegration of existing political structures. While some see these trends as contradictory, they are not. There is a search for economic efficiency and growth through the harmonization of economic policies in larger and larger — eventually, perhaps, global — trade and investment blocs, each of which has to be governed by supranational institutions that set and monitor the rules. This necessity is joined with a desire for greater personal security, a sense of belonging, and ultimate social purpose at a more localized and community level.[13]

The compelling logic of centralization of economic policies in supranational institutions coexists with the natural drive toward decentralization of community and political attachments. No one is safe from the impersonal laws and consequences of global competition. Security is sought in the restoration of community values and standards.

Some functions are necessarily delegated upward toward supranational structures — for example, rules governing the free flow of trade, capital, and technology. Other functions may well be delegated down to more local governments, where they can more effectively supply the needs of citizen consumers.[14]

In Canada, forces for political decentralization have been strengthened by the increasing north-south orientation of trade and by the growing constraints on federal fiscal and monetary policy to pursue domestic stabilization objectives.

---

12 See Richard Simeon, "Globalization and the Canadian Nation-State," in G. Bruce Doern and Bryne B. Purchase, eds., *Canada at Risk? Canadian Public Policy in the 1990s* (Toronto: C.D. Howe Institute, 1991).

13 See Richard Gwyn, "Canada at Risk," in ibid., pp. 116–121.

14 For a discussion, see Thomas J. Courchene, *Global Competitiveness and the Canadian Federation* (Toronto: C.D. Howe Institute, forthcoming).

The idea that the federal government was able to manage — which is to say, avoid — international business cycles was very much a part of what postwar Ottawa was expected to do for Canadians. In fact, it was the postwar confidence that domestic monetary and fiscal policies could stabilize western industrial economies that facilitated a return to the pre-Depression world of global trade and financial flows.

Despite its current popular press, global economic integration is not a wholly new concept or a new reality; the first attempt to build an international economy, including the gold standard — the equivalent of a worldwide monetary union — came in the 19th century. That structure was shaken by World War I and finally shattered in the Great Depression of the 1930s. After World War II, the goal of Keynesian national monetary and fiscal policy was to protect us from international business cycles. It no longer can. We need new institutions, but ones that will be international, not national, in scope. There is, for example, already a growing attempt to coordinate macroeconomic policies in the G-7.

Competitive Government

In this context, the future of the federal government will depend on its ability to pursue and strengthen those areas where it is clearly functionally superior — that is, where it is competitive. For example, existing international institutions are in need of overhaul and new ones may need to be created. Macroeconomic policy, regulation of financial institutions, competition policy, and environmental policy are all candidates for improved international coordination and perhaps new transnational institutions. Canada needs a strong federal presence for the promotion, design, and staffing of these institutions.

Part of this is a question of where Canadians believe they fit in the world. Western Europe has 1992 and a vision of embracing the newly noncommunist countries of Eastern Europe. The United States has Mexico and Latin America as an integral part of its vision of the future. Canadians have yet to decide. The role of the federal government will be to provide leadership in developing and promulgating that vision, and to carry out its functional tasks.

There is also the issue of the free flow of goods, services, people, and capital *within* Canada. For years, the issue of interprovincial barriers has been on the national agenda, but little has been accomplished. Federal leadership is the only way in which real progress can be made. Progress on this issue is essential to Canada's international competitiveness, and perhaps to the future of the Canadian polity as well.

The emphasis at all levels of government should be on functionality. What do people value? What can the nation, province, or municipality deliver efficiently and innovatively? These are the questions to which all governments and their leaders must turn. It is particularly critical for a state that has no overarching ethnic, geographic, linguistic, or cultural homogeneity. If the state is to represent shared values, in Canada they will have to be uniquely political ones. Government will find function and purpose (and a vision) in those policies and institutions that reflect these shared political values. Moreover, to endure, government will have to serve these underlying values both uniquely and efficiently. These are issues to which we return in Chapter 5.

3

Perspective on Competitiveness: The Longer-Term View

Why Competitiveness?

In his new book, *The Competitive Advantage of Nations*, Michael Porter says, "The only meaningful concept of competitiveness at the national level is national productivity....Sustained productivity growth requires that an economy continually upgrade itself."[1] In this view, competitiveness is not about trade balances or exchange rates. It is about finding institutional structures and policies that are conducive to the maximum long-term increase in value added per employee.

Investment in the Future

Competitiveness, then, is a long-term issue. It is fundamentally about raising future income per worker. As such, it inevitably involves investment — the sacrifice of the present for the prospect of a better future.

---

[1] Michael E. Porter, *The Competitive Advantage of Nations* (New York: Free Press, 1990), p. 6.

That investment will take many different forms, not just the increase of physical capital in plant and equipment. Often, the greatest potential reward may be from "soft" investments in institution building — for example, in expenditures on research and development, in acquiring knowledge about a market, in building a skilled sales force, in developing a new organizational structure, in designing a new inventory control system, in negotiating strategic alliances, or in acquiring new skills.

These investments may be undertaken and financed by individuals or by organizations. In each case, it raises questions about who will pay and whether private markets alone are efficient mechanisms for producing the best social outcome. Much of Canada's present public policy apparatus is built on these considerations, with subsidies for various forms of personal, family, and corporate investment.

To reiterate, however, this investment process inevitably involves the sacrifice of present consumption for greater future consumption. For public policy to continue to correct for potential underinvestment or to promote even greater investment, there must be consensus about the fundamental importance of this objective to society and to each individual or group that participates in it. Again, this is a question of political values; there is no economic theory which dictates this choice. But there are very important economic, political, social, and decent human reasons for pursuing it.

Indeed, competitiveness can be tied in an important way to Canada's political and constitutional future. Part of the problem is that Canadians must return to the question of shared political values, and to what they want of Canada. Daniel Yankelovich, writing about public values and competitiveness in the United States, suggests that, for Americans, it is a matter of returning to consensus around the concept of equality of opportunity. This is best achieved in a society dedicated to increasing real income per worker (the essence of the competitiveness objective).[2] As U.S. President John Kennedy said, a "rising tide lifts all boats." Low-growth societies are divisive, fractious, and ultimately stagnant and intolerant.

In this country, the federal government has initiated the Citizens' Forum on Canada's future (the Spicer Commission) to ask Canadians directly what values they see in being Canadian. This should be a central component of any future reforms. It has been suggested that, in the past, Canadians have valued political and social stability at least as much, and probably more, than Americans.[3] If this is so, the need to maintain rising incomes, where all have an equal chance to participate, is even more important.

Destabilizing Debt

One of the most immediate economic reasons for pursuing increased real income per worker is the huge external debt that Canada has built up in recent years. There can be no dispute about the burden of this debt on Canadians, both now and in the future. Since 1985, Canada has increasingly relied on foreign savings, and the country's net external debt now approaches $250 billion. At current exchange rates, the real interest rate on this debt exceeds all estimates of projected future real growth potential.

Canada also has a huge internally owned public debt, which has major implications for the future distribution of the burden of repaying it. This is separate from any output losses from the disincentives that the future tax burden of the debt implies. The main point of this argument, however, is that the

---

2 Daniel Yankelovich, "The Competitiveness Conundrum," *The American Enterprise*, September-October 1990, pp. 43–51.

3 See Seymour Martin Lipset, *Continental Divide: The Values and Institutions of the United States and Canada* (Toronto; Washington, D.C.: Canadian-American Committee, 1989); reprinted in a trade ed. (New York: Routledge, 1990).

public debt can become extremely divisive, politically and socially, when it comes time to repay. This is especially the case if the debt has not supported investment expenditures that will increase the real income of Canadians, or does not increase future income in a way that facilitates a wide participation in those benefits. Politically divisive debt burdens have also been the ultimate source of serious inflations.

The importance of economic growth — based on productivity growth — to social and political cohesion is not a new recognition or a new concern. It received widespread attention in the wake of the worldwide productivity decline that began in 1973.[4] Much of the changed attitudes and policy priorities regarding social programs in North America in the late 1970s and throughout the 1980s can be attributed to the underlying resistance to them in the context of much slower real income growth for everyone.[5] That changed attitude has brought needed reform and more may be required, but it is possible to go too far. A reform agenda should not be extended to the point of denying social need.

Social Progress

Despite its derogation in some quarters, the greatest social program yet invented was not a government program at all. It was the enormous expansion of the private economy and of North American productivity growth in the 1950s and 1960s. The root causes of poverty in our society may not be directly resolvable by economic policies, but they are easier to deal with in a progressive and wealthy community. Full employment —

---

4 See, for example, Lester C. Thurow, *The Zero-Sum Society: Distribution and the Possibilities for Economic Change* (New York: Penguin Books, 1981).

5 See Thomas J. Courchene, "Toward the Reintegration of Social and Economic Policy," in G. Bruce Doern and Bryne B. Purchase, eds., *Canada at Risk? Canadian Public Policy in the 1990s*, Policy Study 13 (Toronto: C.D. Howe Institute, 1991), pp. 125–148.

an excess supply of opportunity — has proven to be by far the best way to lift people up over a long period of time so that they can experience the enormous capital gain of self-worth.

In last year's *Policy Review and Outlook*, Tom Courchene quoted Senator Daniel Moynihan as saying that "the United States has become the first society in history in which the poorest group in society are the children, not the aged."[6] Courchene went on to suggest that this was an apt description of Canada as well. While Courchene's argument was related to a justification for the cutback of Canada Pension Plan payments to higher-income elderly, an increasing number of children do live in poverty conditions, often with single mothers. This is a time bomb for the future, and one that a society that sees itself as investing in the future, in competitiveness, should address with some urgency.

It may be that a labor market that is increasingly divided between "good" and "bad" jobs, as well as the increase in the number of "bad" jobs — characteristics of which include low incomes, tenuous labor force attachment, and part-time employment — can be largely explained by demographics.[7] If so, the problem ultimately may resolve itself through slower labor force growth and an aging society. But it would be foolish to believe that there are no long-term adverse consequences if many people find themselves in an environment in which there appear to be few opportunities for real advancement. A competitive society would address this issue.

It is well known that Canada's population structure is aging. Future generations of working Canadians will bear a substantial tax burden to provide even the current level of

---

6 Thomas J. Courchene, "Social Policy," in Thomas E. Kierans, ed., *Getting It Right*, Policy Review and Outlook, 1990 (Toronto: C.D. Howe Institute, 1990), p . 81.

7 See Economic Council of Canada, *Good Jobs, Bad Jobs: Employment in the Service Economy* (Ottawa: Supply and Services Canada, 1990). The Council does not believe the issue is entirely demographic.

income support for the elderly. There is also the enormously higher burden of health-care costs of the elderly. Demographics alone do not make this an increasing burden, but costs per patient continue to increase rapidly as health technology advances.[8] What is also significant is the growing disparity in incomes in the current generation of workers — young people have much lower incomes, regardless of region, sector, or occupational group.[9] This increasing income inequality, if it persists, may well result in intergenerational political warfare.

Canada's International Standing

A final reason, but not necessarily the least important one, for pursuing competitiveness is Canada's status in international affairs. The income and wealth of Canadians determines this country's international standing and its ability to shape international institutions to reflect Canadian values. As Canada's relative position in these terms declines, its voice will become less effective. Wealth also gives Canadians options and choices that might otherwise be unavailable.

For those who desire to see standards of living rise throughout the developing world, Canadians' own real income growth is also important. To bring themselves up, developing countries need open access to rich, growing markets such as Canada's. But unless Canada is rich and growing, it will not allow that access, our politics will resist the competition of low-wage labor. Competitiveness will help Canadians to find their way through that moral conundrum.

---

8 The elderly account for about 10 percent of the population, but use more than 30 percent of health-care resources.

9 See John Miles, Garnett Picot, and Ted Wannell, "The Changing Wage Distribution of Jobs, 1981–1986," *Canadian Economic Observer*, November 1988.

An International
Perspective on Productivity

Canada is a high-productivity, high-income country. Yet others in the international community are rapidly gaining ground and have all but caught up in productivity terms. Productivity growth in the United States and Canada has lagged substantially behind that in Japan and Europe, as shown in Table 3. But it is important to put this development into perspective.

International Convergence

Some of this relatively poor North American productivity growth is explained by catch-up on the part of economies with substantially lower aggregate productivity levels (and real incomes). The gap in productivity levels between North America, Europe, and Japan was enormous following World War II. The United States, in particular, began with every advantage: the most up-to-date technology, a huge internal market from which to gain scale economies, little wartime destruction or dislocation, and a workforce of educated young men, many of whom were educated under armed forces programs after the war. [10]

The income and productivity gap narrowed as Europe and Japan rebuilt their devastated economies with the latest technologies and as they gained from growing internal markets and greater access to external markets. Indeed, throughout the postwar period, all industrial economies have been converging at varying rates on the United States — the world's most productive economy.

For the Japanese, the greatest relative gains in productivity growth came in the 1960s, a period in which few argued that

10 Michael L. Dertouzos et al., *Made in America: Regaining the Productive Edge* (Cambridge, Mass.: MIT Press, 1990).

Table 3

Business Sector Productivity Growth in the G-7 Countries, 1960–88

(average annual percentage change)

	1960–73	1973–79	1979–88
	Total factor productivity[a]		
United States	1.6%	–0.4%	0.4%
Japan	6.0	1.5	2.0
West Germany	2.6	1.7	0.8
France	4.0	1.7	1.7
Italy	4.6	2.2	1.0
United Kingdom	2.3	0.6	1.6
Canada	2.0	0.7	0.2
	Labor productivity[b]		
United States	2.2	0.0	0.8
Japan	8.6	3.0	3.2
West Germany	4.5	3.1	1.7
France	5.4	3.0	2.6
Italy	6.3	3.0	1.6
United Kingdom	3.6	1.6	2.1
Canada	2.8	1.5	1.4
	Capital productivity		
United States	0.2	–1.1	–0.4
Japan	–2.5	–3.1	–1.7
West Germany	–1.4	–1.1	–0.9
France	0.9	–1.0	–0.4
Italy	0.3	0.3	–0.6
United Kingdom	–0.6	–1.5	0.5
Canada	0.5	–0.7	–2.0

[a] Total factor productivity growth is equal to a weighted average of the growth in labor and capital productivity. The sample averages for capital and labor shares are used as weights.

[b] Output per employed person.

Source: *OECD Economic Outlook*, December 1990.

relative performance was an issue. North America's own productivity performance was quite strong at that time, affording it the luxury of implementing a significant expansion of welfare state social programs.[11]

Aside from international convergence of productivity levels based on the adoption of best-available technology in Europe and Japan — and in Canada, as it also converged on U.S. productivity levels — there are other important considerations. Both the United States and Canada had very significant postwar baby booms, unlike Italy, France, Germany, the United Kingdom, or Japan, and both experienced very rapid labor force growth beginning in the early 1970s. The catch-up countries did not have to deal with this, but instead had greater incentives to install more labor-efficient technology than did North America.

In short, Europe and Japan have enjoyed high rates of investment in the postwar era, with the latest technology — in Europe, much of it from U.S. multinationals entering those markets — and with comparatively slow labor force growth. The fact that they have also had declining capital productivity growth reflects these same conditions. In addition, the very high initial returns to capital that Europe and Japan experienced during their postwar reconstruction have been declining with the progress of economic convergence, international financial integration, and multilateral tariff reduction.

Economic and
Political Conditions for Growth

Historical perspective, therefore, is essential if one is to avoid succumbing to the latest public policy concerns about the

11 Hugh Heclo, "Toward a New Welfare State," in Peter Flora and H.J. Heidenheimer, eds., *The Development of Welfare States in Europe and America* (London: Transaction Books, 1984), pp. 383–406.

supposed economic decline of North America. Yet numerous questions remain unanswered: Why can a lead not be sustained? Since the world's most productive economy, the United States, has extremely weak productivity growth, will all industrial countries now slow to the U.S. growth rate as economic convergence becomes complete? Will the United States be supplanted as the leader? What set of private industrial and political-institutional structures determines the long-term differential growth rates between nations? As Mancur Olson notes,

> estimates of the sources of growth, however meticulous, subtle, and useful, do not tell us about the ultimate causes of growth. They do not tell us what incentives made the saving and investment occur, or what explained the innovations, or why there was more innovation...in one society or period than in another...Neither do they explain the silting up of the channels of economic progress. [12]

The Cold War was an economic even more than a military competition. That struggle apparently has now ended, with the victory of mixed capitalist systems over the Soviet central planning system. Economic convergence is almost complete among Europeans, North Americans, and Japanese. Is a new struggle now under way among Europe, Japan, and North America for economic and technological leadership? If it is, this new economic competition — unlike that with the Soviet Union — would be among essentially equal players (depending on Japan's ability to build its own regional alliance).

These players have essentially similar operating systems, but with some institutional differences that have become major points of international conflict as well as emulation. Each, however, seeks answers to the mysteries of growth and competitiveness. What is the wellspring of growth and competitive-

---

12 Mancur Olson, *The Rise and Decline of Nations: Economic Growth, Stagflation and Social Rigidities* (New Haven: Yale University Press, 1982), p. 4.

ness? And what does all of this mean for Canadian trade, investment, and innovation policies? What does it mean for the activities and structure of government? These issues are addressed in the next two chapters.

4

Prospering in a Global Economy: Trade, Investment, and Innovation Policies

Competitiveness has become the major business issue in Canada. This is largely because of the sharp appreciation of the Canadian dollar, the implementation of tariff reductions under the Canada-U.S. FTA, the rising burden of social regulation, and the slowdown in the domestic economy. These are all immediate concerns driving business interest in this issue. The most perplexing public policy problem, however, may turn out to be the longer-term issue of weak productivity growth. Sooner or later, the productivity problem will translate into a major political issue. The stability of Canada's political, economic, and social structure is predicated on superior economic performance.

This chapter addresses the competitiveness issue from the perspective of productivity growth. The first section reviews the key facts that have formed the backdrop for, and in some cases driven, international trade and investment policy in the 1980s, and that are likely to continue to dominate in the near future.

The next section briefly reviews the relationship of industrial structure — in particular, the transnational or multinational enterprise[1] — to invention, innovation, and trade. This is followed by a look at the implications of this industrial structure for the international trade, investment, and innovation policies pursued by the United States, Japan, and the European Community.

Lastly, the chapter considers Canada's most appropriate policy responses, given both the relationship of industrial structure to innovation and the trade and innovation policies of the other large industrial countries. The conclusion is that Canadian trade, investment, and innovation policy should have four major objectives:

- to gain the widest possible access to foreign markets;
- to constrain, insofar as is possible, the use of strategic trade policies or subsidies by the major industrial powers — in particular, the United States;
- to ensure that Canada is not disadvantaged as a location for foreign direct investment from any nation; and
- to foster a competitive climate that allows the maximum creation of innovative enterprises in Canada.

Trade and Investment in the 1980s

Four important international developments took place in the 1980s to which Canada's trade and investment policy responded and, the Institute believes, must continue to do so. These are:

- the emergence of large international trade imbalances among the three leading industrial countries — the United States, Japan, and Germany;

---

1 The terms "transnational" and "multinational" are used synonymously here. In fact, transnational, multinational, global, and international are sometimes used to distinguish different corporate organization structures, principally in terms of the degree of decentralization of strategic business decisions and assets.

- growing protectionism among all members of the GATT, as well as increased resort to unilateral trade policy actions by the United States;
- the further development of regional trading blocs in North America and Western Europe, coupled with the nascent development of a Western Pacific bloc; and
- the very rapid growth, in the latter part of the 1980s, of European and Japanese multinational corporations, with particular emphasis on entry into North America.

Trade Imbalances

Much of the international debate about macroeconomic, trade, industrial, and competitiveness policies, as well as much of the heat of domestic and international political discord, can be explained by reference to the emergence in the 1980s of the enormous U.S. trade deficit and corresponding trade surpluses of Japan and Germany.

In gross terms, there is every reason to believe that the U.S. trade deficit has more to do with that country's macroeconomic savings imbalance than with unfair trading practices or the strategic trade policy actions of Europe or Japan. U.S. domestic spending simply outstripped the ability of the U.S. economy to supply those demands.[2]

˙ The excess total consumption over production has found its microeconomic expression in those sectors — such as autos and consumer electronics — where foreign competitors have significant advantage in terms of quality products. U.S. firms have either exited — to focus on more profitable businesses — or surrendered significant shares of the domestic market.[3]

---

2 See Richard G. Lipsey and Murray G. Smith, *Global Imbalances and U.S. Trade Policy: A Canadian Perspective* (Toronto; Washington, D.C.: Canadian-American Committee, 1987).

3 For a review of several industries, see Michael L. Dertouzos et al., *Made in America: Regaining the Productive Edge* (Cambridge, Mass.: MIT Press, 1990).

In addition, however, U.S. exporters have been constrained
by lack of market growth — due to excessive debt — in their
traditional export markets in Mexico and Latin America. In fact,
U.S. policy increasingly will be directed to restoring those
markets — as witnessed, for example, in the willingness of the
United States to consider the Mexican free trade initiative.

Growing Protectionism

Whatever the cause of the current international trade imbalances, the situation has greatly enhanced the political prospects
for protectionism. That protection, known as "administrative
or contingent" protection, has taken the form of the increasing
use and misuse of antidumping, countervailing duty, and
escape-clause actions, all ostensibly legal under existing GATT
rules. Indeed, it has been suggested that these protectionist
actions have been "privatized" in such a way that they are now
instruments of private corporate strategy.[4]

"Managed trade" — such as voluntary export restraints —
has also flourished, as has the resort to "unilateralism" on the
part of the United States as it tries to pry open foreign markets
through bilateral negotiations to remove structural impediments to trade. The increased targeting of subsidies to "strategic" industries or firms in high-technology areas is another
potential major source of international dispute. The Uruguay
Round of GATT negotiations was in part an attempt to address
these growing concerns about the inadequacy of existing GATT
rules and procedures for dealing with the new pressures for,
and new forms of, protectionism.

---

4 See Patrick A. Messerlin, "The Antidumping Regulations of the European
  Community: The 'Privatization' of Administered Protection," in Michael J.
  Trebilcock and Robert C. York, eds., *Fair Exchange: Reforming Trade Remedy
  Laws*, Policy Study 11 (Toronto: C.D. Howe Institute, 1990), pp. 107–139.

The Uruguay Round, Regional Blocs, and Mexico

Notwithstanding the advantages for all players in strengthening and extending the GATT regime, there is a distinct possibility that the Uruguay Round will fail. As of early February 1991, the talks have been postponed indefinitely.

The key stumbling block is agricultural subsidies. These are massive; they are producing huge distortions in world production and trade, and are adding to the fiscal problems of governments. Yet these issues are also deeply rooted in domestic politics, for all sides. The European Community (EC) is especially reluctant to make concessions on agricultural subsidies that are acceptable to the other major participants. However, whether this single issue, out of 14 substantive areas of reform, is sufficient to scuttle all progress depends on the options and consequences for each side.

In the case of the EC, it may see itself increasingly as having many more options. It has continued to develop a wider and deeper internal trading bloc under the *Single European Act —* Europe 1992. It also now has potential access to a large pool of low-wage labor in Eastern Europe; it has powerful incentives to support economic expansion there, both as a market for Western Europe's high-value-added goods and services and to make large-scale Eastern European migration to the West unnecessary. Accordingly, the EC may not be inclined to make politically painful concessions in the GATT talks, even under strong pressure from the United States. If so, a satisfactory conclusion to the Uruguay Round may not be forthcoming.

Japan, on the other hand, does not have as many options at the moment. Like most Pacific Rim countries, Japan is still deeply tied to the U.S. economy, through both trade and investment. Notwithstanding suggestions of the possibility of a Japanese-dominated Western Pacific bloc, there is no immediate likelihood of this forming.

The real showdown, then, is between the United States and the EC, with a very important role played by the smaller and less-developed countries with agricultural interests. And the question is: Should existing positions on agriculture be allowed to scuttle the other major advantages that agreement would provide? No one can be certain of the answer, but reason would suggest some compromise by both sides. The Uruguay Round promised to strengthen substantially the existing machinery to resolve trade disputes and to introduce important disciplines in "new" areas — such as services, intellectual property, and investment — that are especially relevant to the sale of higher-value-added goods and services. These would be very significant gains for all developed, industrial countries; to lose them would be illogical. To obtain such gains, however, the developed countries must be prepared to take on the politics of domestic agriculture and to reduce substantially subsidies to local production. The EC must decide where its future growth potential is greatest.

While the failure of the Uruguay Round would be a setback for world trade, it would not be a disaster. It would not mean the end of GATT nor would it necessarily represent any retreat from international commitment to the existing set of trade rules. Moreover, progress continues to be made on bringing down trade barriers independently of the GATT. The EC continues to make huge strides to integrate its internal market. The unification of East and West Germany already represents an important expansion of that common market. Similarly, the United States and Japan have engaged in negotiations that should lead to a reduction of trade barriers and trade disputes. The U.S. Structural Impediments Initiative, involving talks with Japan, was completed in June 1990 with a series of commitments by both sides. Some of these commitments relate to the macroeconomic savings and investment issues discussed above. Others are more strictly structural in that they are directed to opening up Japan's market to exports and further foreign direct investment by addressing exclusionary and preferential business arrangements that are embedded in the structure of the Japanese economy. Canada must also seek opportunities to continue to make progress. Enhancing Canada's status as a location for investment depends on increasing and securing access to as many markets as possible. This, plus the benefit of bargaining power, means that the best route for Canada is to stick with the GATT as the preferred mechanism for trade policy. Failing that, however, Canada has to be prepared to continue to press its interests bilaterally or in a smaller group of countries.

Canada's decision to seek to join the U.S.-Mexico trade initiative is consistent with that strategic thinking. It does not diminish in any way this country's commitment to the GATT, since that commitment is based, at least in part, on Canada's negotiating advantages from participation in multilateral talks. The trilateral initiative would, however, maintain Canada's competitive position relative to the United States in the Mexican market. In the beginning, this would be a negligible advantage, but Mexico's 85 million people and rapid labor force growth rate represent a huge potential market, especially as enhanced trade access to the United States raises Mexicans' real incomes.

Canada's participation would also equalize the advantage — stemming from access to low-cost Mexican components — that the United States would have in competing with Canadians in the U.S. market. In short, Canada's participation would help to avoid the possible emergence of a "hub-and-spoke" model for regional trade liberalization, in which one country — in this case, the United States — gains preferential locational advantage by having separate preferred access to each of its regional partners through exclusive trade pacts with each.[5]

---

5 See Ronald J. Wonnacott, *U.S. Hub-and-Spoke Bilaterals and the Multilateral Trading System*, C.D. Howe Institute Commentary 23 (Toronto: C.D. Howe Institute, 1990).

Such an arrangement would enhance the United States as the most preferred investment location in the bloc.

Foreign Investment in North America

Accompanying the growth of huge international payments imbalances in the 1980s was a very rapid expansion of foreign direct investment, much of it by the Japanese and Europeans (see Table 4). Most of this investment was directed at North America.[6]

There are several explanations for this phenomenon. In part, it might be seen as a natural development of business strategies in industries characterized by substantial investments in "soft" or intangible assets (see below). It may also, in part, have been a counterattack against the invasion of Europe by U.S.-based multinational firms in the 1950s and 1960s. In the late 1980s, the substantial depreciation of North American currencies *vis-à-vis* the Japanese and some European currencies undoubtedly was an added motivation for direct investment, both in making North American assets cheaper and in making the alternative export strategies more difficult. The inflow of foreign direct investment into North America may also have been a precautionary move against growing U.S. trade protectionism.

The influx of foreign investment, however, has created its own protectionist reaction in the United States, manifest in attempts to screen and/or prohibit foreign takeovers. Some of the political reaction has taken the form of pointing to the involvement of foreign — particularly Japanese — corporations in the U.S. political process.[7] This U.S. reaction represents a

---

6 See Investment Canada, "International Investment: Canadian Developments in a Global Context," Working Paper 1990-VI (updated) (Ottawa, November 1990).

7 See, for example, Martin Tolchin and Susan Tolchin, *Buying into America: How Foreign Money Is Changing the Face of Our Nation* (New York: Time Books, 1988).

Table 4

**Outward Flows of Direct Investment from
Major OECD Countries, 1971–80 and 1981–88**
(cumulative percentage shares)

	1971–80	1981–88
United States	44%	22%
United Kingdom	18	21
Japan	6	17
Netherlands	9	7
West Germany	8	9
France	5	7
Canada	4	5
Sweden	2	2
Other OECD countries	4	10

Source: Organisation for Economic Co-operation and Development, Department of Economics and Statistics.

potential opportunity for Canadians to continue to appeal as a stable and hospitable production base in North America, but this depends on further action under the Canada-U.S. FTA, an issue to which we return below.

Global Industrial Structure and Innovation

Innovation

Virtually every definition of competitiveness implies a continuous upgrading of the quality and/or uniqueness of goods and services. At the core of this upgrading is innovation. Productivity improvement comes in this case not simply from more efficient or larger-scale production, but primarily from the continuous introduction of new and/or more sophisticated products — so-called higher-value-added products. Michael Porter has noted:

> Innovation...is defined broadly to include both improvements
> in technology and better methods or ways of doing things. It
> can be manifested in product changes, new approaches to
> marketing, new forms of distribution, and new conceptions
> of scope.[8]

Just-in-time inventory control in Japanese auto plants is an
example of a major productivity-improving innovation.

Global Industrial Structure

As a result of the postwar opening of international markets to
world trade and the continued expansion of multinational
enterprise, a new global industrial structure is developing. It
is hierarchical, and a few large players dominate: the top 600
transnational corporations, all with sales of over a billion
dollars, account for 20 percent of total value added in manufacturing and agriculture in market economies. Moreover, they
account for a substantial portion of world trade and much of
its patentable technology.[9] The top firms participate in many
national markets, with substantial market shares in each, and
they usually sell many related products or product lines.

The next tier consists of players that are medium sized.
They are also multinationals, but they sell in fewer national
markets. Each has fewer products and typically a smaller
market share in each product than the top transnational
corporations. Next are threshold or would-be multinational
companies. Finally, there are the purely domestic or, perhaps,
regional companies, usually with only one or two major products. Regardless of size, however, each firm employs a different
corporate strategy, depending on the mix of resource constraints and opportunities it confronts.

8 Michael E. Porter, *The Competitive Advantage of Nations* (New York: Free
Press, 1990), p. 45.

9 United Nations, Centre on Transnational Corporations, *Transnational Corporations in World Development: Trends and Prospects* (New York: United
Nations, 1988), pp. 34–36.

Advantages of Size

The unique features of multinational industrial and service corporations — as opposed to resource corporations — is that they compete in industries that employ relatively large amounts of "soft" or intangible capital — primarily investments in technical, legal, marketing, financial, or administrative knowledge. [10] These soft assets are, of course, the "source" of innovation, high productivity, and higher-value-added goods and services.

In the hierarchy of firms in these industries, there are substantial barriers to upward mobility, primarily related to financing high-risk soft investments in competition with major established players. For example, high levels of risk are often coupled with huge development and manufacturing costs or with heavy fixed costs in marketing and distribution. Financing for these costs may not be available to smaller enterprises.

Large firms may also enjoy economies of scale in production, marketing economies from multiproduct output, and economies from learning by doing. The combination can lead to strategic advantages to being first in an industry, then using the various economies to gain critical cost advantages over would-be entrants.

The Importance of Market Share

Firms in industries characterized by multinational corporate strategies typically compete strongly for market share. [11] This behavior is not, however, inconsistent with maximizing returns. These competitors seek to earn large returns on their investments in knowledge. The more markets and the larger

---

10 See Richard E. Caves, *The Multinational Enterprise and Economic Analysis* (Cambridge: Cambridge University Press, 1982).

11 Peter Drucker refers to this business objective as a "new reality." See Peter F. Drucker, *The New Realities* (New York: Harper & Row, 1989).

the market share in each, the greater the return to an innovative idea, especially if learning by doing has also lowered production costs. To earn these high returns, however, firms must be able to defend their market share against potential new competitors, either by legal or economic barriers. Therefore, in practice, it may be difficult to separate returns to anticompetitive behavior from those available to innovative behavior.

Sharing Rewards

Evidence suggests that owners of these firms do not capture all the extra returns, but that employees also share in them.[12] In fact, it is likely that some of the extra profits never accrue to the firm or its employees, but instead are dispersed more generally to key suppliers and local service industries that provide financial, legal, technical, and administrative support.

There may also be benefits to the community beyond this redistribution of the gains to innovation or monopoly. Firms in industries characterized by the use of multinational corporate strategies tend to cluster in specific geographic locations and to create a critical mass of positively reinforcing activities that may yield generally available social benefits.[13] All of these factors suggest the importance to a nation's economic prospects of being a favorable location for multinational enterprise.

The Relationship among Trade, Investment, and Innovation Policies

Wide access to foreign markets, through trade or direct investment, allows maximum returns to innovative concepts, ser-

12 Lawrence F. Katz and Lawrence H. Summers, "Industry Rents: Evidence and Implications," *Brookings Papers on Economic Activity* (Microeconomics 1989): 209–275.

13 Michael Porter, for example, emphasizes "clustering." See Porter, *The Competitive Advantage of Nations*.

vices, or products. These gains are potentially continuous and go beyond the once-and-for-all productivity improvements that are available as a result of traditional trade-related increases in production efficiency or scale economies. The production of high-value-added, tradable goods and services has another advantage, in that it facilitates the traditional gains from open trade with low-wage countries. Yet, because this source of comparative advantage is not dependent on low labor costs, it allows for continuously rising labor incomes in the mature industrial economies. It is the benefit of trade without direct competition.

Unfortunately, the type of international industrial structure described above readily encourages certain types of economic policy response. Models have been developed that imply a potential welfare gain to an activist industrial policy based on selective subsidization.[14] The policy proposals that have come out of these models have drawn empirical support, at least on an anecdotal basis, from the apparent experience of Japan and the possibility of "created" comparative advantage, whereby investment in selected export industries leads to high productivity growth.[15]

U.S. Trade and Innovation Policy

There is a temptation to believe that an activist industrial policy is an old and largely discredited idea, and that is certainly true in Canada. In the United States, however, it is still something relatively new. It is also something relatively urgent and rivet-

---

14 For a general discussion of industrial policy in small countries, see Richard G. Harris, *Trade, Industrial Policy and International Competition*, Royal Commission on the Economic Union and Development Prospects for Canada Collected Research Studies 13 (Toronto: University of Toronto Press, 1985), chap. 7.

15 See Richard G. Lipsey and Wendy Dobson, eds., *Shaping Comparative Advantage*, Policy Study 2 (Toronto: C.D. Howe Institute, 1987).

ing, since it relates to the question of the waning dominance of the United States in international affairs. [16] For Americans, this issue is very much tied up with the U.S. trade deficit, with increasing foreign ownership of U.S. industry, and with U.S. concerns about European and Japanese attempts to subsidize selective industries and technologies. The United States' desire for global technological supremacy is also very much involved.

Recently, U.S. antitrust law has been relaxed to allow for various cooperative research programs between firms under the *National Cooperative Research Act.* As well, U.S. defense spending on technology — under the Defense Advanced Research Projects Agency in the Department of Defense — now emphasizes the importance of commercial technologies to defense applications; it also emphasizes the importance of commercial markets to maintain the financial strength and viability of defense contractors. When coupled with recent protectionist trade policy initiatives, these facts suggest that the United States may now be inclined toward a more activist industrial policy model. [17]

Canadian International Trade and Investment Policies

For Canadian public policy, the issue is not so much to rehash the same old debate, but to understand how the interaction of theory, fact, and ideology is influencing the trade and investment policies of the world's major industrial economies. It is in

---

16 For a useful discussion of these issues in the United States, Europe, and Japan, see Sylvia Ostry, *Governments and Corporations in a Shrinking World: Trade and Innovation Policies in the United States, Europe and Japan* (New York: Council on Foreign Relations, 1990).

17 Ibid., pp. 61–75. Recent initiatives include the U.S.-Japanese Semiconductor Agreement, and the formation of a joint government-private sector corporation to develop new production processes for manufacturing semiconductors.

relation to these developments that an appropriate Canadian policy response must be framed.

There are dangers to Canada's industrial structure if the United States further succumbs to the concepts of an activist industrial policy. As the United States refocuses its defense spending, and if it takes up the challenges — real or imagined — of European and Japanese technological advances, the emergence of "strategic" industry subsidy wars becomes a real possibility. The basic political, bureaucratic, emotional, and even theoretical conditions are there to support this type of policy approach in the United States.

Dangers to Canadian Policy

For Canada, however, there are three very strong arguments against an industrial policy that uses targeted subsidies or other protectionist devices:

- first, and most important, is the risk that other governments will retaliate, leaving all players worse off;
- second, while large countries may have to worry about failing to respond to foreign subsidies, for small countries the cost of competitive subsidies is likely to be so substantial that they will be outbid in these competitions in any case; and
- third, there is almost no way in which purely political considerations can be separated from the choice of target industries or firms.

Canada cannot win this game. It should therefore develop less targeted and less overtly hostile ways to become a favorable location for the more innovative sectors of the global economy. Moreover, Canada's interests lie in restricting, as much as possible, the use of subsidies or trade policy by the large industrial countries to attract or retain firms in innovative industries.

The general proposition can be simply put. For those international players with less economic and political power to pursue strategies or games that accentuate the use of such powers is surely self-defeating. That small nations often succumb to these strategies is testament to the political attractiveness of selective subsidies. Yet the result of selective subsidy games is more likely to be gross overcapacity for everyone, domestic political and international discord, and eventually an unsustainable position for the smaller countries.

The FTA and Secure Access

In a number of respects, the Canada-U.S. FTA was as much about investment as it was about trade. Indeed, tariffs were already quite low between the two countries. And while tariff reduction nominally gives Canada greater access to the U.S. market, the question remains as to whether that access is politically secure. Political manipulation of trade policy rules, even though legal under the GATT, raises barriers to trade through increased uncertainty and the added cost of legal defense against arbitrary actions.

In the FTA negotiations, the primary Canadian objective was to ensure that, insofar as offshore foreign direct investment is seeking a North American location to supply the North American market, it would not be discouraged or disadvantaged by U.S. trade laws or policy from locating in Canada. This objective was of particular relevance given the specific context of significantly increased European and Japanese investment in North America. Secure access and the mitigation of U.S. protectionist actions would, of course, also reassure existing North American firms about using Canada as a location from which to export to the United States.

Secure Access: Progress to Date

Secure access, as such, is an objective that can never be fully accomplished. No democratic system could achieve a situation in which resort to the political process was not a strategy open to those feeling the pressure of economic loss. Even economic union does not achieve that situation. Moreover, growing U.S. resentment about foreign investment shows that equal treatment is not necessarily assured to foreigners, even by investing directly in the United States. Nonetheless, the proximate objective of secure access is to streamline the trade-adjudication process and to make it open and subject to agreed-upon rules to the maximum degree possible. Institutional progress toward this objective has been made under the FTA, but more is necessary.

One measure of progress has been the establishment of a mechanism for binational panels to review determinations (under U.S. or Canadian law) to ensure that antidumping or countervailing duties are applied according to respective national laws and on the basis of the facts. The panels' decisions are final and binding on both parties.[18]

To date, the process has gone relatively smoothly. There have been 11 countervail and antidumping cases; only one of these was against Canada, and it was dropped. In the others, the U.S. Commerce Department was either upheld or required to make adjustments. Some observers believe, however, that the real test of the FTA's dispute machinery will come over the alleged subsidies to Canadian pork producers and processors.[19] In that case, the U.S. determination of subsidy was

---

18 Other secure access provisions include panels to make recommendations on general trade disputes relating to the FTA; provisions restricting the use of special safeguard quotas or penalty duties; and a provision for specifically naming the other country in any changes related to the countervail and antidumping laws.

19 See Gordon Ritchie, *Making It Work: Year Two of the Canada-U.S. Free Trade Agreement* (Ottawa: Strategicon Inc., 1990).

found to be inconsistent with the GATT, the subsidy calculation has been questioned under an FTA panel review, and the International Trade Commission finding of injury to U.S. producers was rejected by yet another FTA panel. The question now remains as to what the U.S. response will be.[20]

Unfinished Business

The fundamental principle of secure access between Canada and the United States requires resolution of issues related to the definition of trade-distorting subsidies, and the political use of countervailing and antidumping duties. During the initial bilateral negotiations, these matters proved to be too contentious to reach agreement. Chapter 19 of the FTA therefore provides for further bilateral negotiations specifically on these issues over a period of five years, with a possible two-year extension. If no agreement is reached by then, either side is free to terminate the FTA on six months' notice.

Having failed to make the fundamental progress it sought with the United States in the initial round of the FTA, the obvious way for Canada to proceed on U.S. trade remedy laws was through the Uruguay Round of the GATT. The FTA uses and builds on existing GATT standards; if the GATT reaches agreement on a new code for subsidies and trade remedies, it would then become part of the FTA machinery.

The bilateral talks, however, should now take on new urgency. If the Uruguay Round fails, Canada should proceed, once again, to press the United States on a new regime to cover antidumping and countervailing duties. The general objective should be to restrict subsidies as much as possible. Moreover, the rules should apply to all forms of assistance, whether or not the goods have crossed national boundaries. This would address the fact that subsidized goods sold domestically can

---

20 The softwood lumber case, discussed below, could be another key dispute.

inhibit imports, a much more important U.S. advantage in the existing situation. Finally, countervail law should reflect net subsidy calculations. Under these laws, subsidies are now calculated only on the offending imports, not on the domestic industry. Fairness and logic dictates that this be rectified.

During the FTA debate, there was concern that Canada would lose the ability to pursue industrial policies — particularly subsidies to key industries. As argued above, however, this approach favors big countries. In general, Canadian interests lie in international rules that restrict the use of subsidies as much as possible.

The basic principles outlined above are reflected in Canada's proposals to the Uruguay Round. In fact, it is difficult to find substantive criticism of the general goals of Canadian trade policy. As is often the case, however, the issue may be in the final accomplishment and the price paid.

There is a myth in the United States that it does not subsidize. This, of course, is not true — much U.S. subsidization is hidden in defense spending or takes place at the state and local level.[21] But U.S. mythology might be a powerful negotiating advantage for Canadians. For Canada to be publicly aggressive in its attempts to restrict the use of subsidies may give it more leverage in a bilateral negotiation.

The issue of the use of antidumping machinery will be difficult for Canadians, since it is much more actively used in this country than in the United States. As practiced in trade law, however, antidumping has a dubious theoretical foundation and, most often, may be simply an administrative device to restrain normal, healthy competition. Accordingly, dumping is more appropriately dealt with under competition law, where anticompetitive behavior can be more rigorously determined and its likely impact assessed. This would require an integra-

---

21 See Murray G. Smith, "Overview of Provincial and State Subsidies: Their Implications for Canada-U.S. Trade," *International Economic Issues* (April 1990), pp. 1–24.

tion of quite different U.S. and Canadian competition law, but
these differences could be bridged. Competition law is clearly
a better test of unfair business practices than are current trade
laws.[22]

Resources, Trade, and Competitiveness

Nowhere are Canada-U.S. trade relations more important or
more contentious, even with the FTA, than in the resource-
intensive sectors of the economy. Potentially one of the most
serious disputes in this area involves the softwood lumber case,
at the heart of which lies the issue of resource pricing.

The U.S. industry had alleged Canadian subsidization of
softwood lumber exports to the United States in 1983. At that
time, however, the U.S. International Trade Administration's
decision found Canadian stumpage practices not to be coun-
tervailable. This decision was reversed in 1986, and in 1987
the two countries signed a Memorandum of Agreement that
resulted in Canada's imposing a tax on softwood lumber
exports to the United States. Since export taxes are prohibited
under the FTA, the Memorandum put softwood lumber outside
its rules. Canadian agreement to the Memorandum was an
expedient move, arguably to aid the larger FTA negotiation. In
any event, it is now imposing significant hardship on the
Canadian softwood lumber industry. The rationale and the
evidence for a countervailing duty were always of dubious
validity, and should be reviewed as quickly as possible.

Aside from softwood lumber, the general issue of resource
pricing looms as a unique trade policy issue for Canada.
Economists argue that the failure on the part of government to
collect full resource value is not a trade-distorting subsidy. It
will not result, for example, in uneconomic timber being har-

22 C.W. Goldman, "Free Trade and Competition Law" (Notes for an address on
the Canada-U.S. FTA, Toronto, March 9, 1990).

vested and sold. So whether Canada does or does not collect full resource revenues should not be a trade issue — as long as subsidies are not given to harvesting, transporting, or processing. The U.S. position in the Uruguay Round, however, is that only resource rights sold at auction would be free from challenge. This would represent a significant change in Canadian practice. It would also raise some interesting questions — for example, with regard to the industrial use of water, particularly in U.S. agriculture. These water rights are not sold at auction. Indeed, this issue raises a whole related set of complex problems with respect to pollution standards and the use of market mechanisms for pricing public resources such as air and water. Further research and clarification is needed in this area to determine appropriate rules.

Canada has a clear competitive advantage in resource-based industries. With the exception of autos, its major export industries are resource based. Natural resources have helped this country to achieve one of the highest per capita real incomes in the world. However, the dominance of resource industries is sometimes implied to be an indication of a structural problem.

Some discussions of competitiveness have adopted the analogy of the nation as a holding company.[23] Each nation has a portfolio of industries that is reviewed for key growth and value-added characteristics. Resource concentration is considered a potential problem because it is expected that the income gains from resource ownership will diminish. Presumably, this results from the fact that resources will become more and more costly to extract, while the number of viable alternative suppliers and substitute materials increases.

It is surely premature simply to accept this view of the resource sector. Resource companies do face cost and compe-

---

23 See, for example, Alan M. Rugman and Joseph D'Cruz, *New Visions for Canadian Business: Strategies for Competing in the Global Economy* (Toronto: Kodak Canada, 1990).

tition problems and a long-term decline in relative prices, but so do all other potential sources of income — such as technological innovation. The issue may be the inventiveness with which new uses are found for old resources. Again, the answers to these complex questions require more research.

Canadian Innovation Policy

There is no preferred portfolio of Canadian exports or composition of Canadian industry. What works is what is competitive, high value added, and undergoing continuous productivity growth from innovative business concepts. This is true whether it is resources, services, or manufacturing. Nonetheless, in the past, special attention has been paid in Canada to the relationship of research and development (R&D) and "high-technology" industries to productivity growth.

As measured by the percentage of its gross domestic product spent on scientific research and development, Canada has a weak science and technology base compared with other OECD countries. This poor Canadian R&D performance is a result of the country's industrial structure. First, the presence of foreign subsidiaries reduces the comparative share of spending on R&D, since, in most cases, such activities are most heavily concentrated in the home country, principally in nearby U.S. locations. Second, Canadian industry is dominated by resource companies, which tend not to engage in significant amounts of R&D, as well as by other low-R&D-intensive manufacturers. Third, the bulk of Canadian R&D spending is concentrated in a few large enterprises.

These facts have been reviewed extensively in the literature on this issue. The only question now is whether any new public policy proposals can be derived from them, or from the continuing development of the global industrial structure described earlier.

The objective is clear: Canada needs to participate in those industry niches that are based on high-value-added goods and services and that are sold internationally. This is best accomplished by maintaining a domestic business climate that is both attractive to multinational enterprise and conducive to the development of indigenous innovative enterprise.

The Importance of Competition

The ultimate question is: What set of domestic institutions will nurture competition? With regard to the role of science and technology in the development of new products and industrial processes, an extensive literature is devoted to examining the type of market structure — for example, the degree of competition — and the size of enterprise that are most conducive to conducting research and development, to the act of invention, and, ultimately, to exploitation of the innovation in the marketplace.[24]

Views are split on the role of competition in innovation. Some argue the advantages of monopoly or oligopoly; others the advantages of competition. In this debate, it is useful to separate the questions of the firm's size from the structure of the industry — that is, the number of competitors and the degree of competition. Large financial resources are often necessary to absorb the substantial development costs of innovation. But the firm's size *per se* does not indicate the degree of competition it confronts.

To some degree, these differing views on the importance of competition underlay different policy approaches. For Japan, an industrial structure based on *Keiretsu* — a complex web of commercial and financial links between companies — is tied to the idea of a government-sponsored industrial policy based on targeting "strategic" industries for growth. In many respects, European policy may be close to this model as well.

24 See F.M. Scherer, *Industrial Market Structure and Economic Performance* (Chicago: Rand McNally, 1971), chap. 15.

In the United States, an activist antitrust policy has historically been seen as more conducive to innovation — although the European and Japanese models increasingly have their proponents and their popular appeal. Recent empirical research by Michael Porter reaffirms the more traditional U.S. view and emphasizes the importance of strong domestic rivalry between competitors, coupled with pressure from demanding buyers and support from aggressive suppliers.[25] This view is in accord with the Institute's understanding of competitiveness and the importance of maintaining a competitive environment.

Views are similarly split on whether large or small size (in relation to a given task) is important to invention and/or innovation. As in most other areas of economic life, it is likely that different-sized institutions have different comparative advantages — with small firm size being more nurturing of invention (again, size is measured in relation to the relevant industry norm, not in some absolute sense). However, it may be that firms good at inventing products are ultimately not those that are most successful at bringing them to markets (both at home and abroad). What is important for innovation policy is to consider how these functions are linked — issues which are taken up below.

Foreign Takeovers

Recently, a number of Canadian-owned enterprises in high-technology industries have been acquired by foreign companies. Some argue this should not be allowed. Some also believe that a few "big names" of the Canadian corporate family could be the subject of future foreign takeover attempts.[26] What is

---

25 See Porter, *The Competitive Advantage of Nations*, chap. 3.

26 See G. Bruce Doern, "The Department of Industry, Science and Technology: Is There Industrial Policy after Free Trade?" in Katherine A. Graham, ed., *How Ottawa Spends, 1990–91: Tracking the Second Agenda* (Ottawa: Carleton University Press, 1990), chap. 3.

important, however, is not the ownership of the corporation, but the benefits it imparts to Canadians. Canada's current approach to foreign direct investment is the correct one. Investment Canada permits intervention in the case of a large transaction, but it presumes that intervention will not occur. As long as Canadian corporate sellers receive the full value of expected future returns, there is no reason to block such transactions. Indeed, foreign takeovers could be an important linking mechanism of the Canadian industrial structure to the top tier of global competitors. The essential keys are, first, a competitive international market in corporate control, so that Canadian sellers receive full asset value; and, second, a Canadian economy that is conducive to generating a dynamic, self-perpetuating core of innovative businesses.

With regard to takeovers, considerations of competition should be more important than any other structural issue. The way to increase R&D spending in Canada is to foster an indigenous and dynamic corporate research community. This is not achieved by discouraging foreign capital. Inventor-entrepreneurs or their backers should be allowed to get the highest possible return on their creativity or on their financial support of innovative enterprise. This provides the maximum incentive to establish and grow new innovative businesses in Canada. What is important is not any specific assets, but the set of domestic institutions that nurtures the continuous development of new businesses.

The emphasis of policy should not be to cling to what has already been established, but to build an environment that encourages more. If foreign entrepreneurs lack information about Canadian technical abilities and small Canadian enterprises, such information should be made available. If differentials in the cost of capital exist, they should not be because foreign capital markets lack information about Canadian companies or because Canadian public policy restricts capital inflow — specifically, the foreign purchase of Canadian assets.

Innovation policy should provide a positive environment for a dynamic small and medium-sized business sector. Dynamism in this sector would be reflected in many start-ups and takeovers, substantial reinvestment in new start-ups, many failures, and a steadily increasing mass of innovative companies. This is best accomplished by:

- encouraging the development of large communities of scientists, engineers, technologists, and technicians;
- ensuring the widespread diffusion of technological and best-practice information;
- ensuring unimpeded access to capital;
- ensuring the maximum return on their investment to the creators of new enterprises; and
- enhancing Canada's technological infrastructure, including information databases and communications networks.

A central element of this approach is a government willing to invest in providing basic infrastructure in an efficient and innovative way. It does not require more direct subsidization of business.

Concentrating Mass

Strengthening Canada's technological infrastructure should continue to be a priority investment. Such infrastructure is not just laboratories and equipment, but also information, communications, and the legal framework for intellectual property. These are legitimate public goods that could be supplied by government more efficiently and innovatively.

One of the areas of greatest promise for future research is the creation of concentrations of inventive and entrepreneurial activity. California's Silicon Valley is the obvious example, but there are others — including some nascent communities in

Canada. Such regionally concentrated alliances and linkages help to build the mass that can capture the spillover advantages of a community of researchers, marketers, financiers, and managers.

Continued government support for the provision of information on technologies and foreign marketing is also an appropriate priority for future policy. The federal government and some provincial governments have moved increasingly in this direction; it needs further encouragement.

Universities should play a key role in future funding for innovation. The university is a center for research and a magnet for building a mass of researchers, technologists, and technicians. These individuals attract entrepreneurs and capital, and themselves often start small innovation-based enterprises. Further public investment in university research is consistent with the notion of continuing to promote the development of small and medium-sized enterprise.

The concept of a national target ratio for R&D has been raised once again.[27] Realistic targets may be a useful device for encouraging better performance. But they are primarily an attempt to leverage government spending. Therefore, if targets are set, they should be regionally based, not nationally based, and they should be composed of a more complete index of factors that are important to creating a regional "complex" of innovative businesses. The target-index factors should also be performance or output oriented rather than simply input oriented (as is the case with R&D targets). One aspect of performance might be the number of new technology-based start-up companies.

---

27 By the House of Commons Standing Committee on Industry, Science and Technology, Regional and Northern Development, as reported in the *Globe and Mail*, December 13, 1990, p. A7. The Committee also recommended doubling, in real terms, the agencies that fund university research, the Natural Science and Engineering Research Council, the Medical Research Council and the Social Sciences and Humanities Research Council.

Capital Markets

Recently, the greater availability of domestic savings for business capital formation in Germany and Japan has resulted in a lower real cost of capital in those countries than for North American enterprises. As a result, the investment time horizon of North American companies is short relative to Japanese or European firms.[28]

Some have argued that this higher-cost capital, short time horizon, and emphasis on quick payback by North American firms has given a strategic advantage to foreign companies, which can afford to be more patient with investments. Lower-cost capital, therefore, leads to more investment in R&D, marketing, sales distribution, and new plants and equipment. Having deeper pockets allows foreign companies to go after market share aggressively and then out-wait the domestic competition. As their competitors leave the industry, the foreign companies can begin to raise prices. The ability to do this, of course, also depends on the potential for reentry or new entry.

The cost of capital issue is a very important one. Typically, one would expect large firms — particularly multinational firms, regardless of ownership — to have access to international capital markets. Coupled with international financial market integration, this should lead to uniform real rates of interest for all. (Of course, small domestic firms, without access, could still be disadvantaged.)

Nonetheless, international financial markets may be segmented or still not fully integrated with domestic capital markets. Such segmentation may be based on domestic legal or structural barriers to lending to, or taking equity in, foreign

---

28 See G.N. Hatsopoulos et al., "U.S. Competitiveness: Beyond the Trade Deficit," *Science*, July 15, 1988.

enterprises. This segmentation would account for any differences in the cost of capital, aside from tax differentials. To the extent that international financial integration continues to increase, these barriers should diminish, placing all large multinational corporations in more comparable positions with respect to the cost of externally generated finance. Accordingly, no general case exists for further subsidies to capital — certainly not for large transnational firms.

Conclusion

It is important to abandon notions of using strategic trade policy initiatives or selective subsidies to further the interests of a particular industry or firm. In general, the concept of targeting specific enterprises — for example, firms on the verge of becoming international corporations — should be discouraged.[29] It is not that real market barriers to corporate growth and development do not exist, but selective subsidy decisions cannot be insulated from political considerations. Also, the volume of resources required would typically be very large in relation to any conceivable public monies available for such subsidization. And it invites retaliation.

To abandon the more spectacular public interventions of proponents of industrial policy is not to abandon the notion of strengthening the innovative qualities of society. The capital market remains a key question mark. If capital market failures are the reason why middle-sized firms cannot break into the ranks of major international competitors, the problem may be in institutional restrictions on financial participation in equity. Investment in soft assets — knowledge-based assets such as marketing — often carries the same risks for lenders as for

---

29 This approach was recommended in Ontario, Premier's Council, *Competing in the New Global Economy*, vol. 1 (Toronto: Queen's Printer for Ontario, 1988).

owners. This may be an argument for encouraging greater equity participation, or at least removing any existing biases against equity in financial regulations and in tax policy. But this is largely an issue of structural reform, not simply one of more subsidy.

Capital markets themselves are undergoing significant institutional change, innovation, and reform. The steady growth of institutional investors, the increase in private placements, and the emergence of "angel" financing in start-up situations are examples.[30] Private responses to the needs of innovative enterprise may be forthcoming. The Institute offers no specific policy advice. The issue of financing for innovative business should, however, be a part of the continuing review of financial regulation and tax policy in Canada.

---

30 Angels are rich entrepreneurs or, increasingly, corporations that provide private equity financing and business or technical advice to start-up companies.

5

Seeking
Competitive Government

Introduction

Government spending in Canada represents roughly 44 percent of GDP. Among the industrial countries, Canada's ratio is less than that of France, Germany, or Italy, but significantly higher than that of the United States, the United Kingdom, or Japan. But whatever the international comparisons, it is clear that innovation, quality, and efficiency in such a large sector of the economy is vital to Canada's overall economic competitiveness. As indicated in Chapter 1, the federal government has asked the private sector to accept structural change — largely in the name of competitiveness. Now comes an even greater challenge, as governments, at all levels must change.

That will not happen, of course, except under a relentless pressure for reform. Competition produces competitiveness — that is, efficient, innovative organization — in the private sector; there is every reason to believe it will be the inspiration for innovative change in the public sector as well. One source of pressure is citizen disillusion with the quality of service provided by government and a growing repudiation of high

levels of taxation. The other is the potential competition to meet
social needs between different levels of government, as well as
from the private sector, from nonprofit organizations, and from
cooperatives or families.

This chapter addresses some of these issues in a prelimi-
nary fashion. More research and analysis must be done, and
this research should be a high priority for the coming year. The
chapter is organized in four parts. The first deals with the
priority need to reduce the federal deficit and to stop the growth
of the federal debt. The second part raises the issue of the
allocation of spending, taxing, and regulatory functions between different levels of government in Canada. The third part
deals with the need for structural reform of public institutions
— or those receiving public funds — to make them more
innovative and competitive. The specific focus here is on Canada's education and health institutions and their role in the
development of human capital. The final part addresses the
relationship between social regulation and competitiveness,
with emphasis on the need to develop a new public review
process to calculate costs and benefits and to outline alternative ways to achieve the desired result.

Competitiveness
and the Fiscal Framework

The C.D. Howe Institute has warned repeatedly that, since one
of the principal dangers of rising government debt and an
escalating interest-cost burden is the potential loss of fiscal
flexibility to deal with a recession, strong budgetary measures
were necessary to control the federal deficit. Those measures
were not taken, and a recession has arrived. Fiscal stimulus is
no longer an option. The recession must not be used to divert
attention from the explosive long-term issue of rapidly accu-
mulating federal debt. Despite the recession, the federal government must continue with its expenditure-reduction

program. This is not, however, to reject the contribution that fiscal policy could make to economic stabilization. As a longer-term initiative, therefore, the Institute has proposed that the unemployment insurance fund be made a more "automatic" and powerful stabilization tool.

A Deficit-Reduction Track

The Institute has also developed its own deficit-reduction program, [1] a core assumption of which is that there will be no further increases in taxes. Given this assumption, and given the Institute's outlook for national income, inflation, and employment, the deficit is unlikely to be reduced in fiscal year 1991/92. The situation is, however, expected to improve sharply in subsequent years.

In 1992/93, for example, the government is expected to be in a position to make a very large reduction in its deficit — about $11.5 billion — as a result of lower interest rates from its anti-inflation policy and the impact of economic recovery on the UI account and on general revenues — which have an increased elasticity as a result of previous tax reforms. The Institute's deficit-reduction targets average $4 billion per year over the subsequent three years. Under this deficit-reduction program, the net debt-to-GDP ratio peaks in 1991/92, as the federal government planned in February 1990.

The target deficit-reduction track will be an important element in containing the expansion of the growing tax burden. As taxes increase as a share of GDP, each additional dollar is likely to have a greater negative impact in distorting efficient economic behavior, thereby lowering economic output.

---

1 Irene Ip has reviewed the historical development and rationale for federal expenditures in various areas. On the basis of this review, she has developed new constant dollar per capita expenditure-reduction targets. See Irene K. Ip, *Strong Medicine: Budgeting for Recession and Recovery*, C.D. Howe Institute Commentary 27 (Toronto: C.D. Howe Institute, 1991).

The Structure of Government

Structural reform of government in Canada inevitably raises a number of questions. What activities can government efficiently undertake? Which level of government should undertake these activities? How should these activities be carried out — through direct provision by government agencies, Crown corporations, regulation, direct subsidy, or contracting out? Such questions speak to the very heart of the role of government in Canadian society, as well as to Canada's constitutional structure. In many instances, there are no definitive answers. Nonetheless, the current public dissatisfaction with government and the continuous wrangling between federal, provincial, and local levels government suggest that competitiveness considerations should be reflected in any reform program.

One area of prime importance to a competitiveness agenda is the need to remove internal barriers to trade in this country. Despite years of discussion, however, progress has been painfully slow and inadequate. What is now required is to address these barriers under the umbrella of an independent national agency patterned to reflect the basic principles embodied in international trade agreements.[2]

In addition, a decision should be made on the appropriate assignment of an overarching regulatory authority — on such issues as product standards, professional standards, financial and communications regulation, to name but a critical few — to facilitate the free movement of goods, services, labor, capital, and information across the country. "Europe 1992" should provide a useful benchmark against which to measure Canadian performance, but it should be possible for Canada to go well beyond what will be accomplished there. The prime min-

2 For a brief discussion, see Robert C. York, "Structural Policy," in Thomas E. Kierans, ed., *Getting It Right*, Policy Review and Outlook, 1990 (Toronto: C.D. Howe Institute, 1990), chap. 3. See also John Whalley and Irene Trella, *Federalism and the Canadian Economic Union* (Toronto: University of Toronto Press, 1986).

ister has recently indicated that this is an area where the federal government might seek expanded powers in return for devolution of other powers to the provinces. This would be an important, competitiveness-oriented approach to the rationalization of federal-provincial powers.

The federal government now spends roughly $25 billion on transfers to the provinces for health, postsecondary education, social assistance, and equalization. These federal programs are supported by federally raised tax revenues and federal borrowing. They have been subject to frequent change, depending on the fiscal circumstances of the federal government. In these changes — in the federal government's move to "block-funding" to replace cost-sharing, for example — consideration also has been given to the lack of incentives for efficient spending behavior by the provinces.

The changes in the last federal budget to health, postsecondary education, and social assistance transfers have once again substantially reduced funding to the provinces, and again in response to the federal government's own fiscal problem. While these transfers are federal programs, the provinces have vigorously objected to the cuts.

As the provinces' own fiscal situations worsen, they are forced to raise taxes. Over time, therefore, the federal government has less and less leverage on the Canadian economy and perhaps less relevance to the Canadian public — to the extent to which this is measured in terms of spending power. For many Canadians, this federal-provincial conflict may seem merely to be shifting the buck, and all bucks come out of their pockets anyway. But there are important competitiveness issues involved.

The time has come to bring even more fundamental efficiency considerations into intergovernmental fiscal relations. A primary consideration should be that the level of government responsible for making spending decisions should also be the one publicly responsible for raising the necessary taxes. This simple linkage would go a long way to addressing some basic inefficiencies in the current incentive structure of intergovernmental fiscal transfers and the allocation of responsibilities for program delivery at the provincial and local levels. For example, the tax room to finance health and welfare might be transferred to the provinces. There is, as well, another model in which federal transfers might go directly to individuals, to purchase those services considered appropriate. Federal funds for training and postsecondary education might fit this model well, especially given the high mobility of skilled labor in Canada.

An essential purpose of any change would be to ensure that the public had a clearer ability to assess whether or not they get value for money — and which government was responsible. As well, the idea would be to make governments less inclined to attempt to lever each other's decisions to join projects for which they actually have a low priority, or to consent to program designs that do not reflect constituent needs or desires. Another purpose would be to encourage greater efficiency and innovativeness in those institutions that supply public services, an issue to which we now turn.

Competitiveness and Human Capital

Economic Security and Competitiveness

It has been a fundamental tenet of postwar economic policy that no market is more important than the labor market. Economic performance cannot be regarded as acceptable, socially or politically, unless the performance of the labor market is acceptable. Through the 1950s and 1960s, Canadian economic policy was directed to ensuring this performance. Macroeconomic stabilization policy and social policy focused on the provision of economic security, through ensuring a high and stable level of employment but also in developing a social "safety net". The system was a kind of mutual insurance umbrella that came to include health care as well.

The development of this postwar social safety net was driven not only by concerns for social justice, but also by the conviction that it was good economics.[3] For one thing, it fit the then-current notions of Keynesian fiscal policy and the need to ensure adequate levels of consumer demand. The principles of government-sponsored unemployment insurance and health insurance were also embedded in sound economic rationales, based on the failure or high transaction costs of private insurance markets.

The social policy system eventually came under attack, however, for its own ineffectiveness and inefficient incentive structures. For example, the provision of social insurance programs (such as unemployment insurance and health-care insurance) have significant redistribution effects in their premium structures (if premiums are used at all). It was recognized that private market failures, often a justification for government intervention, had their counterparts in government failures to supply services efficiently. These attacks on inefficiencies in the provision of public services gained momentum after the sharp showdown of productivity growth in 1973. Those concerns continue to plague the current system and are compounded by the emergence of large budgetary deficits and high taxes. The public's desire for economic security remains, however, and national macroeconomic stabilization policy has become less and less viable.

As indicated in the opening chapter, competitiveness is a way to achieve economic security. Yet social policy spending is increasingly seen as at the expense of economic growth and efficiency. Tom Courchene has pointed to the need to reintegrate social policy with good economics. If such a reintegration can be made, it has its greatest prospect in the areas of

---

3 See Thomas J. Courchene, "Toward the Reintegration of Social and Economic Policy," in G. Bruce Doern and Bryne B. Purchase, eds., *Canada at Risk? Canadian Public Policy in the 1990s*, Policy Study 13 (Toronto: C.D. Howe Institute, 1991), chap. 9.

education, training, health, and the provision of efficient programs of social insurance. Investment in ourselves is the first
building block and the ultimate purpose of economic progress.

Knowledge is power, and developing the ability to acquire
knowledge is the essence of Canada's educational system.
Education is an asset the personal economic payoff of which
is not fully reflected even in income statistics. Education allows
for more informed choice and provides options that the uneducated cannot even imagine. To have a poverty-level income
and to be uneducated or illiterate is, in this society, to be truly
without means.

Good health is equally essential to full human development. Canada cannot become a highly dedicated, highly
trained, high-income society without also being a healthy one,
emotionally and physically. Moreover, the two are mutually
reinforcing — high income and social status lead to better
health.

Health and education are sectors of massive government
involvement in Canada, as they are to varying degrees else-
where in the world. Government is involved in influencing
decisions with respect to both the supply and the demand
(through setting prices) for these services. Efficiency, quality,
and innovation in these sectors will be central to Canada's
future growth potential. The Institute is not proposing that
more funds be devoted to these sectors, but that a detailed
review of the incentives embedded in their current organizational structure first be undertaken. The focus that follows is
primarily on the supply side — the efficient provision of public
services. But there are, as well, major issues related to whether
these services are properly priced.

Quality Education and Skills

Recent reports on labor market policy accept the need for
Canada to participate in the international economy through

the production and exchange of high-value-added goods and services.[4] At present, that participation is based on the multinational enterprise, often very large and either Canadian or foreign owned. The industries in which they compete are characterized by the use of knowledge and information, and exhibit high levels of innovative activity. They employ people with high skills and educational qualifications. In part, this is because they are knowledge-based industries, but it is also because educational qualifications are a useful screening device for access to these jobs. Employees in these firms increasingly require "high-flex" skills, which are essentially strong basic learning abilities, a willingness to change, and an ability to work in teams. The high-value-added service industries — engineering, finance, business, and law — that are closely associated with the manufacturing sector have similar educational and skills requirements.

The more high-wage, good jobs Canada has the better. Accordingly, the most important set of public policies will be those that increase the capacity of the high-value-added sectors to expand. That depends not just on the firms actually engaged in international competition, but also on the competitiveness of the institutions that supply them. Increases in the quality of education and the speed with which Canadians learn or acquire new skills — compared with people in other industrialized countries — could be a source of unique advantage. To gain this advantage requires a renewed attention to the competitiveness of Canada's educational institutions. The focus should not be whether enough is spent on education, but on whether Canadians are getting an efficient and innovative education system.

---

4 See, for example, Canada, Advisory Council on Adjustment, *Adjusting to Win* (Ottawa: Supply and Services Canada, 1989).

Elementary and Secondary Schools

By international standards, Canada invests heavily in education, being second only to Sweden among OECD countries in 1985. Yet an increasing number of performance criteria indicate the need for quality improvement. Among the indications are the following:

- Close to one-fifth of the adult population is functionally illiterate — that is, reading at or below the grade 9 level.
- A relatively high secondary school dropout rate — nearly 30 per cent — coupled with a scarcity of apprenticeship and training programs means that more Canadian young people are falling outside the formal education and training system than is the case for the youth of many of Canada's competitors. For example, only 72 percent of Canadian 17-year-olds participate in a formal education or training program, compared with 87 percent of Americans and 94 percent of Japanese.
- Although Canada has a high postsecondary attendance rate, some studies suggest that one reason for this is a relatively less demanding postsecondary curriculum than that of many other countries.
- Canada has failed to rank above the middle level in several international comparisons of student achievement in mathematics and science.
- A disturbingly high proportion of those taking trade and vocational programs do not appear to benefit from their education. Graduates experience high unemployment rates and low average earnings, and the majority report that they do not use the skills acquired in their studies.
- By some international standards, the quality of the high-skill segment of the Canadian work force is only mediocre. According to the 1989 World Competitiveness Scoreboard, Canada ranks in the middle group with respect to managerial talent, research and development personnel, and skilled labor.[5]

Some of these problems may reflect the need to invest even more in education, perhaps much more than other countries,

5 Harvey Lazar, "Investing in People: A Policy Agenda for the 1990s," in Doern and Purchase, eds., *Canada at Risk?*, pp. 158–160.

given the multicultural and diverse linguistic backgrounds of Canadians. But part of the problem may be the need for structural reform of the education system itself.

If the focus shifts to issues of quality, then the first institutional change would be to endorse basic standards and a system of accountability for meeting these standards. The Ontario Premier's Council has recommended the implementation of a core curriculum in language, maths, and science as a "platform for life long learning," to be reflected in a common curriculum for all students up to grade 10.[6]

The second structural change would be to make educational institutions accountable for their results. The Premier's Council noted that:

[policy] should emphasize educational standards and evaluations by introducing:

- a sampling system to monitor educational standards;
- province-wide benchmark evaluation to cover basic skills;
- comprehensive profile assessments for students;
- an annual report card to the public to identify achievements and progress.[7]

The monitoring and testing would become measures of performance of "the system", not just of the students. In the context of competitiveness, these are examples of useful and timely proposals for reform.

Postsecondary Education

The issues of institutional reform extend beyond the secondary school system to include skills-training programs and postsecondary institutions such as universities and colleges. The

---

6 Ontario, Premier's Council, *People and Skills in the New Global Economy* (Toronto: Queen's Printer for Ontario, 1990), p. 27.

7 Ibid., pp. 41–43.

many insightful reviews and useful suggestions for reform in these areas should be given high priority on the public agenda, especially those with a focus on building competitive institutions in the public or private domain. Given the importance of postsecondary education to Canada's competitiveness and to Canadians' sense of economic security, any reform or rationalization should be comprehensive.

One possible course of reform would be to convert all federal funding for postsecondary education and training into vouchers that could be used in any domestic institution or approved program of postsecondary training, anywhere in the country. Since postsecondary institutions and programs — government funded or private — would then have to compete for students and their vouchers, there would be a powerful incentive for rationalization and quality improvement. Such a reform might also be integrated with individual tax incentives or the UI program to take account of the need for lifelong learning and the growing prospect of frequent career changes.

Among postsecondary institutions, the universities are perhaps the most urgently in need of rationalization and reform. They have suffered a significant decline in real funding per student over the past few years, and other social spending initiatives — such as health, welfare, and the environment — will continue to encroach on their public funding.[8] The time has come, therefore, for this sector of the economy to be deregulated. The exact dimensions of this deregulation — specifically with regard to overall student tuition fees, and fee differentials between different programs of study — should be the subject of critical review in the coming year. There are other issues as well, related to whether all or some universities should be deregulated, to the role of colleges and other private training programs, and to whether the federal government

---

[8] For a discussion of this issue, see George Pedersen, "The Challenge for Universities," in Doern and Purchase, eds., *Canada at Risk?*, chap. 12.

should play a more direct role, through the vouchers mentioned above, in financing access to postsecondary education. In this review process, the analysis should be on freeing up competition.

Quality Health Care

By international standards, Canada spends a lot on health care. In fact, it is second only to the United States in health spending as a percent of GDP. Yet the health of Canadians is not significantly better than — or, in some cases, even as good as — that of people in other industrial countries. Accordingly, this fact alone should raise questions about the efficiency of Canada's health system.

At the same time, it is apparent that, relative to the U.S. system, some aspects of the Canadian system do provide a significant cost advantage to Canadian enterprise and to the Canadian economy. Levels of health do not appear to be materially different between the two countries — by some measures, such as infant mortality, Canada does significantly better. Yet Canada spends substantially less of its national income on health care than does the United States — about 8.7 percent compared with 11.2 percent. Moreover, the Canadian system provides universal insurance coverage with no price barriers to access; 15 percent of the U.S. population still has no coverage whatsoever.[9]

Despite the apparent cost competitiveness of the Canadian health-care system relative to that of the United States, the rising proportion of health expenditures in provincial budgets — it is now over one-third — and high costs relative to other industrial countries indicate the need for continued improve-

9 For a brief review of Canadian health-care issues, see Robert Evans, "Health Care: Is the System Sick?" in Doern and Puchase, eds., *Canada at Risk?*, chap. 16.

ment. The list of inefficiencies in the Canadian system that could be addressed by institutional reform is long: inefficient incentive structures in hospital-funding mechanisms; inefficient payment schemes for doctors; ineffective or even dangerous medical procedures; excessive use of medical technology; and excessive testing and over-prescription of drugs.

The provinces control the supply of health care. They are also responsible for its organization and delivery — setting hospital standards, regulating fees and salaries of health-care workers, and administrating health insurance. All provinces recognize that providers need to be more accountable for health expenditures, and that the system needs to be managed more actively. There is widespread recognition of the need for a focus on maximizing health outcomes, not inputs. It is also recognized that health is affected by a wide range of policies other than expenditures on health care.[10] The problem will be to develop allocation mechanisms that can actually make the tradeoff of less money for active-care programs and more for sickness-prevention programs.

Each province has become involved in its own health-care review process. Many new experiments are taking place in all areas. This activity should be encouraged and accelerated as part of a program of competitive government. As well, an important area of potential cost increase is the manner in which compensation rates are set for all health-care workers, not just physicians. The issues are complex — and include most public sector employees. In health care, compensation is often determined by compulsory arbitration, and in some cases, the legislation is antiquated and in need of review and reform.

---

10 For the development of a broader framework for health policy, see Robert G. Evans and Greg L. Stoddart, *Producing Health, Consuming Health Care*, Centre for Health Economics and Policy Analysis Working Paper Series (Hamilton, Ont.: McMaster University, 1990), pp. 90–96.

Competitiveness and Social Regulation

The Economic Burden of Government

It was argued above that government delivery of public services makes up such a large part of the economy that innovation and improved efficiency in government are essential to promote greater overall productivity in the Canadian economy. Where government is particularly efficient, it is likely to be a unique source of cost advantage relative to other jurisdictions — health care in Canada versus the United States, for example.

Government is even more pervasive, however, in its ability to regulate and set rules in society. The federal government's recent moves toward deregulation have been in economic areas dealing essentially with output, price, and entry restrictions in certain industries. At the same time, regulation has increased in social areas such as employment standards, occupational health and safety, pay and employment equity, and the environment. Much of this increased regulation, in fact, has come at the provincial level. Even though most regulatory activities of government are based on widely shared public values, their implications in terms of costs and efficiency of implementation are rarely known or understood, even by government.

Business now feels particularly vulnerable to these government-imposed costs, primarily because of the rising value of the Canadian dollar, high interest rates, and squeezed profit margins. The impact of tariff reductions under the Canada-U.S. FTA has also played a role in heightening business concerns. The loss of cost competitiveness from increased regulatory costs may cause some Canadian industries or firms to move to locations in the United States. This is particularly germane in the current context of a widespread rationalization of North American production facilities in multinational firms.

In general, two clear cost concerns are related to more regulatory activity. One is the increase in costs relative to those for competing suppliers in other jurisdictions. The issue here is simply whether Canadians understand and are prepared to accept the costs of getting substantially ahead, in government-dictated social standards, of competitors in nearby industrial jurisdictions. In a competitive environment, that cost is not borne solely by business, but also by those whose jobs may be in jeopardy in the high-productivity, high-wage sectors to which these standards usually apply. The second, related issue is the potential inefficiency of regulations in reaching least-cost solutions to the problems they are meant to address. This represents a clear excess burden of government.

The Environment and Efficient Instruments

Environmental regulation is an area where government policy objectives often can be achieved more efficiently by appropriate policy design, thereby minimizing the social burden of government. For example, the introduction of markets and prices for permits to emit pollution is one mechanism by which greater efficiency — as well as higher levels of environmental protection — can sometimes be achieved.[11] This is the approach that the United states has adopted in its recent clean air legislation. Where it is neither feasible nor efficient to establish markets, pollution taxes may be a preferred substitute to existing command-and-control regulations.[12]

In either case, the prices of permits or the taxes would be a first approximation of the social costs of using environmental resources such as air or water. There are indications that the

---

11 See, for example, Arlon R. Tussing, "Environmental Policy Issues: Market Failure in the Third Phase of Economic Activity," in G. Bruce Doern, ed., *The Environmental Imperative: Market Approaches to the Greening of Canada*, Policy Study 9 (Toronto: C.D. Howe Institute, 1990).

12 See Nancy Olewiler, "The Case for Pollution Taxes," in G. Bruce Doern, ed., *Getting It Green: Case Studies in Canadian Environmental Regulation*, Policy Study 12 (Toronto: C.D. Howe Institute, 1990), chap. 8.

public would support having to pay higher prices for environmentally friendly products and, specifically, that it would support the concept of "let the polluter pay."

The enormously complex and contentious process of setting pollution standards and monitoring compliance is not made easier by these market-pricing or tax mechanisms. But the introduction of environmental prices and costs into Canadian production and consumption decisions would lead to a reduction in pollution and to a more efficient use of public resources.

Setting Standards

Setting standards is always a difficult social issue, and often a complex economic, scientific, medical, and legal one as well.[13] The economic complexity is compounded by the need to look at the standards of competing jurisdictions. In these instances, there is an incentive for Canadians to pursue international agreements that raise all standards. In an integrated world economy, international cooperation is also the challenge of those who seek social progress. Acid rain, for example, is a clear case where Canadians were instrumental, and ultimately successful, in the introduction of an environmental initiative in the United States. Canadian policy should be to promote collaborative progress with relevant competing jurisdictions.

The Need for Independent Regulatory Review Agencies

As a practical matter, it would be virtually impossible to determine whether Canadian environmental and social regulation, on balance, involved greater efficiency costs than the

---

13 For a discussion of the process, see G. Bruce Doern, "Social Regulation and Environmental-Economic Reconciliation," in Doern and Purchase, eds., *Canada at Risk?*, chap. 7.

total of similar regulations in relevant competing jurisdictions. Moreover, the degree to which some regulations substitute for more costly government programs would have to be reviewed — for example, occupational health and safety regulations should reduce the outlay on medical care. Other effects, such as the impact on innovation, should also be considered. For example, efficient environmental regulation can be the basis on which new industries and new products are born.

It should not be presumed that a conflict is inevitable between social regulation and economic efficiency, innovation, or growth. By the same token, it should not be presumed that economic growth is inimical to social and environmental progress. For example, wealth and economic security are the greatest single determinants of human health, both physical and emotional. The point is that, given all of these complexities, it is important to have a thorough and public review of the impact of regulatory policies on Canadian competitiveness before they become law.

Ultimately, the choice of regulatory instrument is a function not simply of the efficiency of that instrument in achieving its objective, but also of the institutional structures and political environment in which decisions are reviewed and made.[14] There is no single institutional structure for best ensuring that the political process yields a policy that delivers the greatest social welfare, but public information, which is nonpartisan, can help. Public knowledge of the cost and benefits of a proposal and the alternatives will help to direct government to the least-cost solution.

There is, therefore, a case to be made for establishing independent regulatory review agencies at both the federal and provincial levels of government. Such agencies would, first, assess the costs and benefits of any proposed initiatives,

---

14 See Michael J. Trebilcock et al., *The Choice of Governing Instrument* (Ottawa: Economic Council of Canada, 1982).

whether environmental, social, or economic; and, second, review alternatives to achieve the same goals. The agencies would provide the information to the public and to committees of government, following the initial introduction of legislation into the federal Parliament or provincial legislatures. Staff for these agencies could be reassigned from existing departments or ministries.

This function is not unlike those now performed inside government in central agencies, usually finance departments or treasuries. There are important advantages to be gained, however, by separating the economic assessment of regulations, their implementation, and their alternatives from purely financial budget issues. There are also advantages in making these assessments publicly available.

Conclusion

Government inevitably must be a part of a competitiveness agenda in Canada. This does not mean that government should design a new industrial policy for the private sector. It means that government and government-funded institutions, at all levels, must become more efficient and more innovative.

It is difficult to imagine a more debilitating problem than the current federal deficit. While it may weaken Ottawa in constitutional negotiations, it is not a constitutional but an economic and political problem. There is hope, however, that continued expenditure restraint — as outlined by the Institute — a much improved inflation and interest-rate environment, and the impact of recent tax reforms will generate a significant improvement in the federal fiscal situation in fiscal year 1992/93. Beyond that, the elimination of the federal deficit should remain a priority objective of a competitiveness agenda.

The public sector in Canada is deeply involved in the supply and pricing of many vital public goods and services — especially at the provincial and local levels. The supply of health care, education, police and fire protection, sewers, roads, highways, and civil law are all functions that are central not only to Canada's international competitiveness, but also to the basic quality of life of Canadians. Government also controls access to and pricing of important natural resources such as forests, minerals, oil and gas, and fish. As well, government must decide how to make the most efficient use of "environmental" resources such as air and water. Government is also the provider of major social insurance programs such as UI, health insurance, and worker's compensation. And none of this even begins to delineate the pervasive role of government in regulating economic and social behavior.

Are Canada's governments and institutions doing all of these things efficiently and innovatively? If not, why not? Can there be internal reform? If not, are there alternative suppliers in the public or private sectors? These are not different questions, nor should they be, than those confronting any competitive firm or industry. But they are the questions that must be addressed.

6

Summary
and Conclusions

No one can deny that these are turbulent, confusing, and sometimes frightening times. A ground swell of fundamental change has begun, both in Canada and throughout the world. For Canadians, this prospect of change is an opportunity as well as a challenge. But to grasp that opportunity and not be overwhelmed by the speed and swirl of events, Canadians must see their current domestic and international circumstances in perspective.

An underlying theme of this *Policy Review and Outlook* has been the need for perspective: on the immediate issue of recession; on recent federal economic reforms; on the convergence of real incomes in the industrialized world to the level of the United States; on the relationship of industrial structure to productivity growth and the implications for innovation, trade, and investment policies in the major industrial countries; and, finally, on Canada's current political malaise in the context of worldwide economic and political restructuring.

Canada is among the world's richest industrial nations. It is reasonably certain that Canadians will wish to maintain that status. But Canada has also accumulated a large debt, both external and internal, that future generations will have to honor. At the same time, Canada is an aging society with a high level of social benefits for the aged. It is also a society in which workers increasingly are polarized into those with good jobs and those with bad jobs. Canada is a rich nation with slowing population growth in a world of wrenching poverty and population explosion. Hope for the Third World lies in trade with, and investment from, countries such as Canada.

Given this economic context, domestic and international political realities will demand that Canadians continue to make strong economic progress in the future. Indeed, there must be significant improvement in the growth of real income per worker over the next decade, compared with the record of the past 15 years. The alternative will be politically and socially divisive, destructive of what we have already achieved, and inevitably would involve a retreat from Canada's international obligations.

This *Policy Review and Outlook* has but one message: Canadian public policy, at all levels of government, should draw its central purpose from the goal of competitiveness. The performance measure of competitiveness is trend productivity growth. Canada's goal should be to improve substantially on its productivity performance of the past 15 years, such that its relative standing in the international community is maintained or enhanced.

While productivity growth is the measure of competitiveness, it is not the meaning of competitiveness. Competitiveness is a structural quality built into Canada's public and private institutions and ultimately woven into its social, economic, and political fabric. Competitiveness reflects relationships built on trust, values, and commitment, an incentive structure dedicated to shared goals, a willingness to accept change, and an ability to innovate.

But competitive institutions do not just happen. Competitiveness depends on competition. Economic efficiency and innovation are the result. This is true of both public and private institutions. Canada must have an economic and political environment that does not, in Mancur Olson's words, "silt up the channels of human progress."[1]

Competitiveness, as a term to describe a public policy objective, has a significant drawback. It implies that people seek competition for its own sake. In their economic lives, however, people seek income, wealth, and security. It is not the means, but the goals, that resonate in popular understanding. Yet these goals can be achieved only through competitiveness. Good public policy must respond to both perception and reality.

Canada's Trade, Investment, and Innovation Policies

An essential element of competitiveness is the ability to innovate — to develop new products and processes. The maximum return to these innovations is earned by having the widest possible access to markets around the globe. Such access has several potential advantages: the traditional efficiency gains from trade and economies of scale; the returns to continuous innovation; the political advantages to industrial nations of not having to compete directly with low-wage labor; and the gains to developing nations of increasing, through trade and foreign investment, the speed with which they develop.

Canada is not, however, the only industrial nation in the world to realize these benefits and to pursue them. Accordingly, Canada's trade, investment, and innovation policies must reflect this fact. They must also take into account Canada's small size relative to the big industrial powers or blocs. Canada must

---

1 For an optimistic assessment of Canada's political economy in this regard, see Robert A. Young, "Effecting Change: Do We Have the Political System to Get Us Where We Want to Go?" in G. Bruce Doern and Bryne B. Purchase, eds., *Canada at Risk? Canadian Public Policy in the 1990s*, Policy Study 13 (Toronto: C.D. Howe Institute, 1990), chap. 4.

seek to restrain the unbridled use of political power in international trade, investment and innovation policies. At the same
time Canada must develop a framework of domestic policies
that promotes competition among its institutions and that
increases the share of the economy involved in the production
of high-value-added tradable goods and services. In short,
Canada's trade, investment, and innovation policies should
have four major objectives:

- to gain the widest possible access to foreign markets;
- to constrain, insofar as is possible, the use of strategic trade
  policies or subsidies by the major industrial powers — in
  particular, the United States;
- to ensure that Canada is not disadvantaged as a location
  for foreign direct investment from any nation; and,
- to foster a competitive climate that allows the maximum
  creation of innovative enterprises in Canada.

To achieve these objectives, the Institute offers the following
recommendations:

Recommendation 1: Since a competitive climate is fostered
by a low and stable rate of domestic inflation, monetary policy
should continue to pursue the goal of price stability by maintaining the annual growth rates of the monetary aggregates M1
and M2 at around 3 percent and 5 percent, respectively.

Recommendation 2: Canada should be a full and active
participant in the U.S.-Mexico free trade negotiations.

Recommendation 3: Canada should continue to press for the
enhancement of secure access in bilateral trade negotiations
with the United States under the FTA.

Recommendation 4: Canada should aggressively seek to restrict the use of subsidies generally, and to get recognition of

the principle of net subsidy in the determination of counter-vailing duties.

Recommendation 5: Canada should seek to integrate its competition law with that of the United States to deal with predatory pricing practices now dealt with under antidumping legislation.

Recommendation 6: Canada should seek to bring the soft-wood lumber case under the terms of the FTA.

Recommendation 7: More generally, Canada should seek to clarify issues related to domestic resource pricing and sub-sidies, including the pricing of environmental resources such as air and water.

Recommendation 8: Canadian trade, innovation, and foreign investment policies should be oriented toward providing a favorable environment for large, multinational enterprises, as well as for a vigorous and growing core of small, innovative domestic businesses.

Recommendation 9: Foreign capital and foreign takeovers should not be discouraged from adding to the potential for developing and expanding the innovative business sector.

Recommendation 10: Competition policy should be pursued aggressively as part of a broader competitiveness strategy.

Recommendation 11: Governments should continue to strengthen the basic infrastructure of, and framework policies affecting, the innovative business sector in Canada. These include the legal framework for intellectual property, the basic research capacity of Canada's universities, and information databases and communications facilities.

Recommendation 12: Targets for innovative activity, including research and development, should be regionalized, broadened to reflect an index of factors affecting innovation, and oriented more toward results — including, for example, new, high-technology corporate start-ups.

Recommendation 13: Financial regulation and tax policy should be reviewed continually to ensure that investment in innovative enterprise is not discouraged or disadvantaged by inefficient or unnecessary regulations for biased tax policy design.

Competitiveness in Government

Competitiveness is not just something for the private sector or those involved in international trade. It benefits all sectors of the economy. To date, many of the federal government's major structural reforms — for example, Canada-U.S. free trade, the GST, and reform of unemployment insurance — have been directed outward to the private sector.

Yet, in many respects, the public has rejected these reforms. This is not, however, because of the objectives or the nature of the reforms. The public's unhappiness is due, in part, to timing — and to the cumulative effects of reform to monetary, trade, and tax policy all at one point. It is also the result of confusion about the effects of structural reform coupled with the cyclical arrival of recession, a confusion promoted by some opponents of the reforms. Bad times are followed by good, however, and circumstances should improve this year as the economy begins to recover, and as Canada's cost performance relative to the United States improves.

Public disillusionment may also stem from the lack of a large-scale effort to cushion adjustment — to the FTA, for example. Indeed, the entire area of human capital investment is one where increased government emphasis and rationalization would reassure all Canadians of their ability to convert the challenge of change into an opportunity for growth.

Recommendation 14: Given the huge importance of human capital to Canada's future competitiveness, and given the sense of security that educational opportunities can give to people confronting change, emphasis should be placed on developing an integrated approach to human capital formation and adjustment. Such an approach would be oriented toward supporting individuals, not institutions or governments, and would include the tax system and some concept of a lifetime of reinvestment and change.

Public disillusionment also may come from the apparent unwillingness of government itself to participate in change by reforming its own institutions and structure — as best exemplified, perhaps, in the public's mind, by the persistence of the federal deficit, notwithstanding a rising tax effort. Accordingly, the time has come for structural reform of government itself. That reform should include all levels of government and all government-funded institutions.

Recommendation 15: The federal government should continue to implement an expenditure-reduction strategy, despite the current recession.

Recommendation 16: Barriers to the free interprovincial flow of goods, services, capital, and labor should be reviewed, with a view to enhancing mobility and creating a stronger Canadian common market.

Recommendation 17: Federal-provincial fiscal transfers should be reviewed with the intention of increasing the efficiency of public sector spending and taxing decisions. At a minimum, this will require linking government responsibilities for spending more clearly with taxing decisions.

Recommendation 18: Efficient and innovative supply of public services requires appropriate internal incentive structures, as well as the external pressure of consumers and competitors. Institutional reform of the education and health sectors, focused on increased quality and efficiency of supply, should be a high priority in the coming year. In education, it means setting a core curriculum and evaluating institutions in terms of results. In postsecondary education, one example of an efficiency-inducing instrument would be to convert all federal support for training and postsecondary education into student vouchers. In health care, efficiency means continual movement away from fee-for-service and toward health-maintenance organizations.

Recommendation 19: The federal government and each province should establish an independent regulatory review agency to assess all regulatory proposals. Such agencies would outline the alternatives, assess the costs and benefits of each, and assess the means by which each could be accomplished. Such reviews would be made public before implementation of the proposed regulation. Staff for the agencies should be reallocated from existing departments or ministries.

Conclusion

In the postwar era, Canadian governments have pursued three broad public objectives: economic stability, economic growth (in real income per worker), and a reasonable degree of equity both between income groups and regionally.

The objective of stability, or minimizing risk, has been pursued through the use of Keynesian macroeconomic stabilization policy, numerous industry-specific stabilization policies (such as agricultural support programs), and various forms of social insurance (such as unemployment insurance). Growth in real income per worker has been sought through industrial policy (that is, targeted assistance to industries and firms) trade policy (through the GATT and the Canada-U.S. FTA), and other "supply-side" initiatives such as tax reform.

Often, however, the design of policies aimed specifically at stability or growth has been infused with the desire for some measure of equity between regions and income groups. The result frequently has been grossly inefficient. An agenda based on competitiveness would begin to sort these issues out, and allow each goal to be pursued efficiently and innovatively.

Once again, Canadians are being asked to debate the constitutional structure of their country. As that debate unfolds, it is important to remember that government is a constituent element of society, constantly reacting and changing as the pressures on it change. Government has a comparative advantage in the supply of public goods, because it can democratically force constituents to pay for those goods. Yet free trade and the increasing mobility of capital and people diminish that advantage. This is a reality shared by all levels of government, not just by nation-states that are struggling for relevance in an integrated international economy.

At the international level, the convergence of real incomes among the major industrialized countries has led to an increasing convergence of their economic policies, particularly tax policies. It has also led to a growing recognition that international collaboration is needed to deal with market failures that the nation-state alone can no longer adequately address.

Governments throughout the industrialized world will continue to evolve to meet these new challenges. But, while collaboration among governments is important, so is competition. Canadians may be dismayed by the degree of federal-provincial wrangling that takes place in this country. They should remember, however, that intergovernmental competition can also serve a useful purpose as a check on the monopoly power of the unitary state.

In 1991, the attention of Canadians will be riveted on the recession, the Gulf War, and the political and constitutional future of the country. Competitiveness, in this context, may seem out of step with popular concerns. Yet the world beyond Canada's borders will continue to unfold, driven by its own relentless economic and political logic. It will not wait for Canadians to resolve all of their differences.

Regardless of how the events of 1991 unfold, the quality of Canada's institutions, their innovativeness, and their competitiveness will determine the country's ability to survive and prosper. For this reason, if for no other, the importance of competitiveness transcends even the most urgent of today's concerns.

Bibliography

Canada. Advisory Council on Adjustment. *Adjusting to Win*. Ottawa: Supply and Services Canada, 1989.

————. Investment Canada. "International Investment: Canadian Developments in a Global Context," Working Paper 1990-VI (updated). Ottawa, November 1990.

————. Royal Commission on the Economic Union and Development Prospects for Canada. *Report.* 3 v. Ottawa: Supply and Services Canada, 1985.

Carmichael, Edward A., and Katie Macmillan. *Focus on Follow-through*, Policy Review and Outlook, 1988. Toronto: C.D. Howe Institute, 1988.

————, Katie Macmillan, and Robert C. York. *Ottawa's Next Agenda*, Policy Review and Outlook, 1989. Toronto: C.D. Howe Institute, 1989.

Caves, Richard E. *Multinational Enterprise and Economic Analysis.* Cambridge: Cambridge University Press, 1982.

Courchene, Thomas J. *Global Competitiveness and the Canadian Federation.* Toronto: C.D. Howe Institute, forthcoming.

Dertouzos, Michael L., et al. *Made in America: Regaining the Productive Edge.* Cambridge, Mass.: MIT Press, 1990.

Doern, G. Bruce. "The Department of Industry, Science and Technology: Is There Industrial Policy after Free Trade?" In Katherine A. Graham (ed.). *How Ottawa Spends, 1990–91: Tracking the Second Agenda.* Ottawa: Carleton University Press, 1990.

————, and Bryne B. Purchase (eds.). *Canada at Risk? Canadian Public Policy in the 1990s*, Policy Study 13. Toronto: C.D. Howe Institute, 1991.

Drucker, Peter F. *The New Realities.* New York: Harper & Row, 1989.

Economic Council of Canada. *Good Jobs, Bad Jobs: Employment in the Service Economy.* Ottawa: Supply and Services Canada, 1990.

————. *Transitions for the '90's*, Twenty-Seventh Annual Review. Ottawa: Supply and Services Canada, 1990.

Evans, Robert G., and Greg L. Stoddart. *Producing Health, Consuming Health Care*, Centre for Health Economics and Policy Analysis Working Paper Series. Hamilton, Ont.: McMaster University, 1990.

Friedman, Benjamin M. "Financial Fragility and the Policy Dilemma," *Challenge*, July/August 1990, pp. 7–16.

Goldman, C.W. "Free Trade and Competition Law." Notes for an address on the Canada-U.S. FTA, Toronto, March 9, 1990.

Harris, Richard G. *Trade, Industrial Policy and International Competition*, Royal Commission on the Economic Union and Development Prospects for Canada Collected Research Studies 13. Toronto: University of Toronto Press, 1985.

Hatsopoulos, G.N., et al. "U.S. Competitiveness: Beyond the Trade Deficit," *Science*, July 15, 1988.

Heclo, Hugh. "Toward a New Welfare State." In Peter Flora and H.J. Heidenheimer (eds.). *The Development of Welfare States in Europe and America*. London: Transaction Books, 1984.

Ip, Irene K. *Strong Medicine: Budgeting for Recession and Recovery*, C.D. Howe Institute Commentary 27. Toronto: C.D. Howe Institute, 1991.

Katz, Lawrence F., and Lawrence H. Summers. "Industry Rents: Evidence and Implications," *Brookings Papers on Economic Activity* (Microeconomics 1989): 209–275.

Kierans, Thomas E. (ed.). *Getting It Right*, Policy Review and Outlook, 1990. Toronto: C.D. Howe Institute, 1990.

Laidler, David E.W., and William B.P. Robson. *Money Talks — Let's Listen!*, C.D. Howe Institute Commentary 26. Toronto: C.D. Howe Institute, 1991.

Lipset, Seymour Martin. *Continental Divide: The Values and Institutions of the United States and Canada*. Toronto; Washington, D.C.: Canadian-American Committee, 1989; reprinted in a trade ed. New York: Routledge, 1990.

Lipsey, Richard G. (ed.). *Zero Inflation: The Goal of Price Stability*, Policy Study 8. Toronto: C.D. Howe Institute, 1990.

———, and Wendy Dobson (eds.). *Shaping Comparative Advantage*, Policy Study 2. Toronto: C.D. Howe Institute, 1987.

———, and Murray G. Smith. *Global Imbalances and U.S. Trade Policy: A Canadian Perspective*. Toronto; Washington, D.C.: Canadian-American Committee, 1987.

Messerlin, Patrick A. "The Antidumping Regulations of the European Community: The 'Privatization' of Administered Protection." In Michael J. Trebilcock and Robert C. York (eds.). *Fair Exchange: Reforming Trade Remedy Laws,* Policy Study 11. Toronto: C.D. Howe Institute, 1990.

Miles, John, Garnett Picot, and Ted Wannell. "The Changing Wage Distribution of Jobs, 1981–1986," *Canadian Economic Observer,* November 1988.

Olewiler, Nancy. "The Case for Pollution Taxes". In G. Bruce Doern (ed.). *Getting It Green: Case Studies in Canadian Environmental Regulation,* Policy Study 12. Toronto: C.D. Howe Institute, 1990.

Olson, Mancur. *The Rise and Decline of Nations: Economic Growth, Stagflation and Social Rigidities.* New Haven: Yale University Press, 1982.

Ontario. Premier's Council. *Competing in the New Global Economy.* Toronto: Queen's Printer for Ontario, 1988.

————. Premier's Council. *People and Skills in the New Global Economy.* Toronto: Queen's Printer for Ontario, 1990.

Ostry, Sylvia. *Governments and Corporations in a Shrinking World: Trade and Innovation Policies in the United States, Europe and Japan.* New York: Council on Foreign Relations, 1990.

Porter, Michael E. *The Competitive Advantage of Nations.* New York: Free Press, 1990.

Ritchie, Gordon. *Making It Work: Year Two of the Canada-U.S. Free Trade Agreement.* Ottawa: Strategicon Inc., 1990.

Rugman, Alan M., and Joseph D'Cruz. *New Visions for Canadian Business: Strategies for Competing in the Global Economy.* Toronto: Kodak Canada, 1990.

Scherer, F.M. *Industrial Market Structure and Economic Performance.* Chicago: Rand McNally, 1971.

Smith, Murray G. "Overview of Provincial and State Subsidies: Their Implications for Canada-U.S. Trade," *International Economic Issues* (April 1990), pp. 1–24.

Thurow, Lester C. *The Zero-Sum Society: Distribution and the Possibilities for Economic Change.* New York: Penguin Books, 1981.

Tolchin, Martin, and Susan Tolchin. *Buying into America: How Foreign Money Is Changing the Face of Our Nation.* New York: Time Books, 1988.

Trebilcock, Michael J., et al. *The Choice of Governing Instrument.* Ottawa: Economic Council of Canada, 1982.

Tussing, Arlon R. "Environmental Policy Issues: Market Failure in the Third Phase of Economic Activity." In G. Bruce Doern (ed.). *The Environmental Imperative: Market Approaches to the Greening of Canada,* Policy Study 9. Toronto: C.D. Howe Institute, 1990.

United Nations. Centre on Transnational Corporations. *Transnational Corporations in World Development: Trends and Prospects.* New York: United Nations, 1988.

Whalley, John, and Irene Trella. *Federalism and the Canadian Economic Union.* Toronto: University of Toronto Press, 1986.

Wilson, Hon. Michael H. *The Budget: Canada's Economic Performance and Prospects.* Ottawa: Department of Finance, February 20, 1990.

———. *A New Direction for Canada: An Agenda for Economic Renewal.* Ottawa: Department of Finance, November 1984.

Wonnacott, Ronald J. *U.S. Hub-and-Spoke Bilaterals and the Multilateral Trading System,* C.D. Howe Institute Commentary 23. Toronto: C.D. Howe Institute, 1990.

Yankelovich, Daniel. "The Competitiveness Conundrum," *The American Enterprise,* September-October 1990, pp. 43–51.

York, Robert C. (ed.). *Taking Aim: The Debate on Zero Inflation,* Policy Study 10. Toronto: C.D. Howe Institute, 1990.

Members of the
C.D. Howe Institute[*]

[*] The views expressed in this publication are those of the author and do not necessarily represent the opinions of the members of the Institute.

Gordon Homer
Honeywell Limited
Hongkong Bank of Canada
Hydro-Québec
IBM Canada Ltd.
Imasco Limited
Imperial Oil Limited
Inco Limited
The Independent Petroleum
    Association of Canada
Inland Cement Limited
The Insurance Bureau of Canada
Interhome Energy Inc.
The Investors Group
Tsutomu Iwasaki
John A. Jacobson
Jarislowsky, Fraser & Company
Robert Johnstone
John Labatt Limited
Lac Minerals Ltd.
R.W. Lawson
Jacques Lefebvre
Gérard Limoges
Daniel Lobb
London Life Insurance Company
Pierre Lortie
Lumonics Inc.
J.W. (Wes) MacAleer
James McAlpine
McCallum Hill Companies
MacDonald, Dettwiler & Associates
    Ltd.
Robert M. MacIntosh
Bruce M. McKay
McKinsey & Company
Maclab Enterprises
James Maclaren Industries Inc.
Maclean-Hunter Limited
Charles McMillan
McMillan, Binch
MacMillan Bloedel Limited
The Manufacturers Life Insurance
    Company

Georg Marais
Maritime Telegraph & Telephone
    Company, Limited
Marsh & McLennan Limited
The Mercantile and General
    Reinsurance Company of
    Canada
William M. Mercer Limited
Merck Frosst Canada Inc.
Metropolitan Life Insurance
    Companies
Midland Doherty Limited
Miles Canada Inc.
Les Minoteries Ogilvie Ltée.
Robert Mitchell Inc.
Mitsui & Co. (Canada) Ltd.
The Molson Companies Limited
Monsanto Canada Inc.
Montréal Trust Company of Canada
W.D. Mulholland
The Mutual Life Assurance
    Company of Canada
NCR Canada ltd.
NEI Canada Limited
National Westminster Bank of
    Canada
Nesbitt Thomson Deacon
Peter C. Newman
Louis-Paul Nolet
Noranda Forest Inc.
Noranda Inc.
Norcen Energy Resources Limited
North American Life Assurance
    Company
North Canadian Oils Limited
Northern Telecom Limited
Northwood Pulp and Timber Limited
NOVA Corporation of Alberta
Ontario Hydro
PanCanadian Petroleum Limited
Peat Marwick Thorne
Lucie Pépin
Charles Perrault
Petro-Canada Inc.

Phillips Cables Limited
Claude Pichette
Les Placements T.A.L. Ltée.
Placer Dome Inc.
Portfolio Management Corporation
Power Corporation of Canada
Prairie Pools Inc.
Pratt & Whitney Canada Inc.
Price Waterhouse & Co.
J. Robert S. Prichard
Procor Limited
ProGas Limited
Provigo Inc.
Quebec and Ontario Paper
    Company Limited
RBC Dominion Securities Inc.
Redpath Industries Limited
Simon S. Reisman
Henri Remmer
Retail Council of Canada
Grant L. Reuber
R.T. Riley
Robin Hood Multifoods Inc.
Rogers Communications Inc.
The Royal Bank of Canada
Royal Insurance Company of
    Canada
Royal LePage Limited
Royal Trust
St. Lawrence Cement Inc.
Sandwell Inc.
Saskoil
Guylaine Saucier
André Saumier
The Hon. Maurice Sauvé
Sceptre Investment Counsel
Sceptre Resources Limited
ScotiaMcLeod Inc.
Sears Canada Inc.
Anthony A. Shardt
Sharwood and Company

Shell Canada Limited
Sherritt Gordon Limited
Sidbec-Dosco Inc.
Smith, Lyons, Torrance, Stevenson
    & Mayer
Le Soleil
Southam Inc.
Standard Life Assurance Company
Stikeman, Elliott, Advocates
Strategicon Inc.
Sun Life Assurance Company of
    Canada
Suncor Inc.
Swiss Bank Corporation (Canada)
Teck Corporation
Téléglobe Canada
Telesat Canada
Thomson Newspapers Limited
3M Canada Inc.
The Toronto Dominion Bank
Toronto Star Newspaper Limited
The Toronto Stock Exchange
TransAlta Utilities Corporation
TransCanada PipeLines Limited
Trimac
Trizec Corporation Ltd.
Robert J. Turner
Unilever Canada Inc.
Urgel Bourgie Limitée
Manon Vennat
Ventures West Management
VIA Rail Canada Inc.
J.H. Warren
Tom M. Waterland
West Fraser Timber Co. Ltd.
Westcoast Energy Inc.
George Weston Limited
M.K. Wong & Associates Ltd.
Wood Gundy Limited
Xerox Canada Inc.
Zurich Life Insurance of Canada

Honorary Members

W.J. Bennett
G. Arnold Hart
David Kirk

Paul H. Leman
A.M. Runciman
J. Ross Tolmie, Q.C.

DATE DUE   L.-Brault

0 1 FEV. 1993		
2 7 NOV. 1993		
5 DEC. 1993		
0 7 FEV. 1995		
2 1 FEV. 1995		